The New York Times

CHANGING PERSPECTIVES

Sex and Sexuality

THE NEW YORK TIMES EDITORIAL STAFF

Published in 2019 by New York Times Educational Publishing
in association with The Rosen Publishing Group, Inc.
29 East 21st Street, New York, NY 10010

First Edition

The New York Times
Alex Ward: Editorial Director, Book Development
Phyllis Collazo: Photo Rights/Permissions Editor
Heidi Giovine: Administrative Manager

Rosen Publishing
Megan Kellerman: Managing Editor
Julia Bosson: Editor
Greg Tucker: Creative Director
Brian Garvey: Art Director

Cataloging-in-Publication Data
Names: New York Times Company.
Title: Sex and sexuality / edited by the New York Times editorial staff.
Description: New York : New York Times Educational Publishing,
2019. | Series: Changing perspectives | Includes glossary and index.
Identifiers: ISBN 9781642821550 (library bound) | ISBN
9781642821543 (pbk.) | ISBN 9781642821567 (ebook)
Subjects: LCSH: Sex instruction for children—Juvenile literature.
| Sexual health—Juvenile literature. | Sexual orientation—
Juvenile literature.
Classification: LCC HQ53.S493 2019 | DDC 613.9071—dc23

Manufactured in the United States of America

On the cover: Times and attitudes have changed, and the
language used to discuss sexual orientation and gender identity
has also changed; Ben Wiseman/The New York Times.

Contents

CHAPTER 3

Queer Identities

CHAPTER 4

Feminism

CHAPTER 5

Sexual Consent and Behavior

Introduction

IN JUNE 2015, the Supreme Court ruled that bans on same-sex marriage were unconstitutional, effectively legalizing gay marriage across all fifty states. The response was tremendous: hundreds of celebrants gathered in Washington, decked out in rainbow garb and chanting "Love has won," and same-sex couples flocked to courthouses across the country, some participating in mass weddings. Millions posted messages in support on social media, using hashtags including #LoveIsLove.

It would be easy amidst these celebrations to forget how quickly cultural attitudes toward sex and sexuality have shifted. Less than half a century prior, not only was legalized gay marriage unthinkable, but sodomy laws were in place across the country, criminalizing same-sex encounters. Transgender individuals had few legal protections and were rarely acknowledged in mainstream culture. And, until the 1970s, a woman could not open a credit card in her name without first obtaining the signature of a man.

The second half of the twentieth century bore witness to a sexual revolution that occurred on several fronts. Not only did gay and lesbian individuals receive wider cultural acceptance and recognition, but women and other sexual minorities found a place for themselves in the mainstream of American society and made headway into achieving equal rights. However, progress did not always follow a clear path: along the way, these pioneers experienced bigotry, hate crimes and legal resistance. However, their work ultimately resulted in a shift of policy, rights and perspectives.

This book is broken into five chapters that show the evolving attitudes toward sex and sexuality: Gay and Lesbian Rights, Transgender Stories, Queer Identities, Feminism and Sexual Consent and Behavior.

Lena Williams, right, and Crystal Zimmer hold hands after they were married at Hamilton County Courthouse in Cincinnati on June 26, 2015.

The reporting on these topics demonstrates the interconnectedness of the lives of LGBT+ individuals and women with the political and cultural gains these groups have made. Our understanding of sex and sexuality is a direct result of minority groups fighting and advocating for equal treatment.

These articles also show how the attitudes of the reporters and the newspaper as a whole have evolved over time. As an article in the first chapter shows, reporting on gay rights in the past featured opinions from psychoanalysts who believed homosexuality could be treated and referred to gay men as "deviates" and "inverts." For many years, most articles on transgender people focused on surgery or violence, sensationalizing but not humanizing transgender issues. And words like pansexual, genderqueer and gender-noncomforming were nowhere in The New York Times' archives.

It is important to note that this title bridges several issues surrounding sex and sexuality. Sexual orientation is distinct from gender identity: while the former has to do with one's attraction to other people, the latter relates to one's understanding of one's own self.

The cultural conversation around sex and sexuality continues to develop with time. In 2017, when news of Harvey Weinstein's history of sexual assault broke, women across the world spoke up as part of the #MeToo movement, elevating the dialogue about gender equality. Sexual assault cases on college campuses raised conversations about sexual consent, and dating apps have changed the dynamics of dating. And the youngest generation has already demonstrated an interest in creating a world without such rigid gender and sexual categories. Ultimately, the individual pieces in this title celebrate the diversity of gender identities and sexual expressions that make up American life and culture.

CHAPTER 1

Gay and Lesbian Rights

In the early morning hours of June 28, 1969, New York City police conducted a raid on the patrons of the Stonewall Inn, a gay bar in the West Village. What followed was a spontaneous riot that became known as the foundation of the gay rights movement. This chapter documents The New York Times' reporting on gay and lesbian rights, demonstrating the growing cultural acceptance of gay identities and evolving editorial attitudes toward how these issues should be covered.

Morals: On the Third Sex

BY MURRAY SCHUMACH | MAY 7, 1967

WHEN WORD GOT OUT last week that Columbia University had become the first collegiate organization in the nation to issue a charter to an organization seeking equal rights for homosexuals, it brought a few rays of sunshine to the twilight world that alternates between the furtive and the flagrant.

And yet, to those homosexuals who have taken considerable risk to try to win for themselves the right to be judged as individuals, it was hardly surprising that this advance — for them — was made in New York City. For it is here that "the third sex" is establishing a national capital.

From the police and the District Attorney's office, as well as from the Mattachine Society, defender of homosexual rights, come reports that the homosexuals find in New York these days more opportunities for employment than they have ever known in this country anywhere. They still find plenty of evidence of discrimination, hostility and harassment, but the climate has improved decidedly. Says an important police official:

> The whole area of morals is a problem and probably always will be. But the situation for homosexuals has improved since last April when we decided that the police were not to be used to entrap homosexuals. I think it has been made very clear to the police that homosexuality is not illegal. A guy can mince down the street with marcelled blond hair and if he doesn't bother anyone it is not illegal. What we get is a steady stream of complaints about such situations.

THE PENALTIES

An experienced prosecutor in the District Attorney's office of New York County believes that "the tendency in recent years here has been to be less severe in dealing with homosexuals." Soliciting by a homosexual is called vagrancy or disorderly conduct, and consensual sodomy among adults is also a misdemeanor, meaning punishment does not exceed a year. Sodomy with a child is regarded as serious, with the maximum punishment 10 years. A child is anyone under 18.

Homosexuals see the improvement in more specific fashion. They note, for instance, that persons taking Civil Service examinations in New York no longer have to say whether or not they are parolees, unwed mothers or homosexuals.

Ironically, like any other group in process of assimilation, the homosexuals who think they are moving toward equality resent the lurid displays by others.

"The mascaraed fagot," says one homosexual, "is just a homosexual derelict." Another says: "Flagrant homosexuals have undoubtedly done us a good deal of harm."

Another self-styled homosexual, Randolph Wicker, who has what he calls the biggest distribution of slogan buttons at 28 St. Marks Place, cites the improvement in bars.

"They used to raid and shut down bars that served homosexuals. Or else there would be 'gay bars' run by underworld characters that catered to homosexuals. Now there are half a dozen private clubs in New York, chartered by the state, run by homosexuals for homosexuals and not harassed by the police if they are orderly."

The Mattachine Society says it has considerable evidence of better job opportunities for homosexuals in New York in advertising, publishing, clergy, teaching and, of course, show business, dress designing, decorating and hairdressing.

"There is a social maturity in New York City toward homosexuals," says a member of this society. "Since Lindsay came into office we've made important breakthroughs in many fields. This increasingly tolerant atmosphere is one reason more homosexuals are coming to New York."

In some respects, even In New York, some of the more far-sighted homosexuals are worried about the future. As corporations become ever larger, they observe, they tend to place greater stress on conformity. And with the enormous advances in computers, nonconformity of any kind can be spotted very rapidly.

"When you already have corporations that deny promotions to men because they have not married by the time they're 30," said a homosexual, "what do you think will happen to us?"

To this, Mr. Wicker responds:

"Things are getting better, in New York anyhow, but none of us is ever going to see the day when we are treated as humans."

'Deviates' and 'Inverts'

BY THE NEW YORK TIMES | APRIL 11, 2009

A "RAINBOW PILGRIMAGE" is what New York City tourism officials call the marketing campaign they introduced last week. The campaign promotes the city "as a rite of passage for the gay and lesbian traveler" and is timed to coincide with the 40th anniversary of a defining moment in the history of gay rights, the Stonewall rebellion.

Before Stonewall — a clash of protesters and the police after a violent raid on a Greenwich Village bar in June 1969 — the city was a gay destination, but certainly not one promoted by its officials, nor particularly welcomed by the wider public. Consider these excerpts from a front-page article in The New York Times in 1963 under the headline "Growth of Overt Homosexuality in City Provokes Wide Concern." The article's language, from sources and reporter alike, is outdated at best, derogatory at worst, and many of its assumptions and assertions are long discredited.

The article draws heavily on a study of gay men by Dr. Irving Bieber, a psychoanalyst who believed that homosexuality was an illness that could be treated or prevented:

> Public acceptance, if based on the concept of homosexuality as an illness, could be useful," he says. "If, by a magic wand, one could eliminate overnight all manifestations of hostility I think there would be a gradual, important reduction in the incidence of homosexuality.

The study also had some ideas about family ties:

> We have come to the conclusion [that] a constructive, supportive, warmly related father precludes the possibility of a homosexual son; he acts as a neutralizing, protective agent should the mother make seductive or close-binding attempts.

The Village, 1969: Near the Stonewall Inn in Greenwich Village on the final night of the disturbances.

Gay marriage was not even a blip on the horizon:

> Many homosexuals dream of forming a permanent attachment that would give them the sense of social and emotional stability others derive from heterosexual marriage, but few achieve it.
>
> The absence of any legal ties, plus the basic emotional instability that is inherent in many homosexuals, cause most such homosexual partnerships to founder on the jealousies and personality clashes that a heterosexual union would survive.

Under the heading "The Borderline Cases":

> There is general belief, however, that strict enforcement of the law against seduction of minors is important to protect borderline cases from adult influences that could swing them toward homosexual orientation when heterosexual adjustment was still possible.

Where and who the "inverts" and "deviates" are:

Inverts are to be found in every conceivable line of work, from truck driving to coupon clipping. But they are most concentrated — or most noticeable — in the fields of the creative and performing arts and industries serving women's beauty and fashion needs.

Some homosexuals claim infallibility in identifying others of their kind "by the eyes — there's a look that lingers a fraction of a second too long."

Most normal persons believe they have a similar facility in spotting deviates.

Homosexuals See 2 Decades of Gains, but Fear Setbacks

BY JAMES BARRON | JUNE 25, 1989

TWENTY YEARS AFTER a police raid on a gay bar in Greenwich Village unleashed the pent-up anger of the homosexual community and started the modern gay-rights movement, homosexual men and lesbians say that laws, court decisions and changing attitudes have helped them move closer to the mainstream of society.

But obstacles remain, along with doubts about when, or if, they will fall. Some homosexuals see what they consider disturbing signs that 20 years of gains are being rolled back under pressure from conservatives and the religious right.

Demonstrations in New York this weekend — a rally in Central Park yesterday, and the annual Lesbian and Gay Pride march today — commemorate the riot at the Stonewall Inn on Christopher Street. That incident, many homosexuals say, awakened lesbians and gay men to the idea that they were being attacked as a group. That, in turn, awakened them to the idea that they needed to organize as a group.

Advocacy and lobbying groups mushroomed after Stonewall, and now include everything from nonprofit groups mounting anti-discrimination advertising campaigns to political action committees.

"For the first time, I think more people are saying, 'I am a human being, I want to take my rightful place in society, I want to be mainstream and I want this aspect of my life to be one of many things of which I am proud,' " said Stephanie Blackwood, a public-relations executive who is leading an advertising campaign to foster greater tolerance toward homosexuals. "I'm about as mainstream as they come, and that's what we want."

LEGAL VICTORIES

To many homosexuals, the last 20 years have seen legal victories, new tolerance by some religious denominations, greater understanding on the part of some heterosexuals and sometimes, action by government.

In 1985, for example, New York City opened the Harvey Milk School in Greenwich Village for teen-age students who say they are homosexuals, and last week, the United States Postal Service announced a special cancellation with the postmark, "Stonewall Sta./20 Years 1969-89/ Lesbian and Gay Pride."

But the evidence is divided on whether society as a whole is now more accepting. Lesbians and gay men say they are still turned down for jobs and housing, even though such discrimination was outlawed in New York City three years ago, and they complain that they must still endure bias and hatred.

The National Gay and Lesbian Task Force reported earlier this month that homosexuals were the victims of more assaults in 1988 than in each of the preceding three years and that antihomosexual violence was "alarmingly widespread." Nineteen percent of those incidents occurred on college campuses, and 17 percent were classified as AIDS-related, "indicating that hatred and blame associated with the epidemic continue unabated," the task force said.

Some gay-rights advocates are concerned that the Republican-controlled New York State Senate, for the third straight year, blocked a bill that would have toughened the penalties for bias-related violence, including crimes against homosexuals as well as against blacks, Hispanic people, women, resident aliens and the elderly.

And a nationwide poll taken in March by The Los Angeles Times found that when asked if they approved of "homosexual rights" — the term was not defined — 51 percent of the 3,583 men and women questioned said they disapproved, while 29 percent said they approved.

That finding was consistent with a nationwide Gallup Poll in the spring of 1987, when Gallup last explored this subject. The survey found that 55 percent were against the legalization of homosexual relations, while 33 percent favored it. Those percentages were about the same as in a 1986 poll that marked the first time a majority had opposed legalization since Gallup started asking the question in 1977, before the AIDS epidemic.

In contrast to the isolation they felt 20 years ago, homosexuals and lesbians now have their own political-action committees, nonprofit foundations and support networks to promote what they feel the heterosexual world is denying them. They have opened community centers with everything from Alcoholics Anonymous to a gay Welcome Wagon. The Lesbian and Gay Community Services Center in Manhattan has a $1.5 million annual budget and 20 meeting rooms.

On the eve of the Stonewall riot there were 50 gay and lesbian organizations nationwide, said John D'Emilio, a historian and a co-author of "Intimate Matters: A History of Sexuality in America," published by Harper & Row. By 1973, there were 800, Mr. D'Emilio said. Now there are more than 3,000. But some gay-rights advocates are concerned that the growth is leveling off. "There's a saturation," Mr. D'Emilio said. "I mean, how many groups can you form?"

Many homosexuals say that all their support groups have helped the movement to downplay the differences among gay people caused by race and gender. So has AIDS.

By pressing lawmakers to allocate money for research on acquired immune deficiency syndrome, homosexuals have become an accepted part of the political landscape, as a bloc of voters if not as elected officials themselves. The staffs of major political figures like Mayor Edward I. Koch and Gov. Mario M. Cuomo now include representatives to the homosexual community. "Gay people are taking their place in the American panoply," said Richard Burns, the executive director of the Lesbian and Gay Community Services Center.

Some now live openly, and comfortably. "I'm more at ease with myself, whereas 20 years ago one had to be much more guarded about how one appeared," said Eric Washington, a waiter and a member of the AIDS Coalition to Unleash Power, or Act-Up. "These days I don't really think about that at all."

At the time of the Stonewall raid, a handful of gay bars, mostly in

Greenwich Village, were among the few places where gay men and women socialized. "We'd carved out a small little world for us, populated by young gay people, which was a happy place, very hip," said Martin Robinson, a co-founder of the Gay Liberation Front in 1969 and of Act-Up in 1987.

The Stonewall Inn was a black-walled bar owned by organized crime. Like a Depression-era speakeasy, it had a peephole in the door and a bouncer who was not afraid to turn people away.

"This was not the polite professional middle-class clientele that worries about making a scene," Mr. D'Emilio said. "Many of them were drag queens, maybe even runaways, so they had less to lose by fighting back."

On June 27 — two months before the rock concert at Woodstock, N.Y., and one month before Neil A. Armstrong became the first person to walk on the moon — the police raided the Stonewall for violations of liquor laws.

"When the police came in," said Mr. Robinson, who was there, "quite to their surprise, we were no longer self-effacing, we were no longer guilt-ridden. We were offended at their bullying. We didn't put up with it. As soon as the police got inside the bar, we surrounded the bar, made it difficult for them to get out."

Michael Scherker, who is writing a history of the events that night, says some people in the crowd threw pennies at the police. Others uprooted a parking meter to use as a battering ram.

"It wasn't a rebellion; it was a plain old spontaneous-combustion riot," Mr. Scherker said. "They weren't thinking of gay rights; they just wanted to get back in the bar. It wasn't until the next day or the day after that or the week after that that a lot of people realized what it was really about was gay rights."

Since Stonewall, even the words society uses to describe homosexuality have changed. The headline on an article that appeared in The Daily News shortly after the riot said, "Homo Nest Raided, Queen Bees Are Stinging Mad."

Now, said Sherrie Cohen, the executive director of the Fund for Human Dignity, "both in the media and society, it's becoming less acceptable to use slang words like homo and faggot against gays." She said the media have begun to reflect "a growing understanding" of lesbians and gay men and issues that concern them.

"This is all to the best in promoting tolerance in society," she said.

The church, too, has struggled with homosexuality. The Roman Catholic Church has not softened its opposition to it, and most Protestant denominations have yet to resolve whether gay men and lesbians can be ministers. But many have tried to bring them into their churches and to make them feel comfortable.

Some homosexuals say nothing illustrates the changes of the last 20 years better than their relationship with government.

"We began by fighting representatives of government," said Virginia Apuzzo, deputy executive director of the New York State Consumer Protection Board. "We still are, in a sense, but I think our demands have changed. The demand at Stonewall was to get off our back. The demand today is not that government should get off our back, but that government should be involved in helping. Now we're saying, 'Government, give us the protections we need to live safely in this society.' "

Some of those protections have come from anti-discrimination statutes that have been passed in more than 50 jurisdictions, including most major cities, said Thomas B. Stoddard, the executive director of the Lambda Legal Defense and Education Fund. And in the 20 years since Stonewall, he said, Federal and state courts have generally supported homosexual plaintiffs in cases in which their rights were challenged. In 1962, seven years before Stonewall, Illinois became the first state in the nation to drop its sodomy law. Since the Stonewall uprising and the evolution of the gay-rights movement, 24 other states have invalidated or repealed their sodomy laws.

The old laws did not prohibit homosexuality per se, but did ban certain sexual acts that Mr. Stoddard said were "rightly or wrongly identified" with gay people, and thus prompted discrimination. In New York, the state's highest court, the Court of Appeals, struck down the sodomy statute in 1980.

But gay-rights advocates are worried about the long-term results of a 1986 Supreme Court decision that upheld the constitutionality of Georgia's sodomy law, saying there was no legal protection for homosexual acts between consenting adults, even in the privacy of their own homes. The Court said the Georgia law forbidding people from engaging in oral or anal sex could be used to prosecute homosexuals who engaged in such acts.

Homosexuals are also concerned that 25 states still have sodomy laws, and that there is no longer much momentum for repeal.

"It's not a good thing it has ground to a halt," Professor D'Emilio said, "but my informed guess is there are far fewer prosecutions. It may not be possible to get a repeal bill through a state legislature, but it is possible to exert pressure on state and local police to keep them from enforcing."

Mr. D'Emilio also argues that the Federal court system is more conservative now because of judges appointed during the Reagan administration, and is less likely to find in favor of homosexuals in discrimination cases.

For that reason, Mr. D'Emilio said, the focus of the gay-rights movement has shifted from the courts to the political system.

"AIDS is an issue of such urgency that it has upped the level of organizing within the gay community and it has opened doors to the gay movement that were not open before," he said. "When the issue was gay rights, if you tried the Federal bureaucracy, the door stayed closed. When the issue is AIDS, the door opens. Gay activists have access to policy-makers in ways that they didn't have 20 years ago."

They also have the Human Rights Campaign Fund, a political action committee that describes itself as the nation's ninth-largest. "Increasingly, congressmen are recognizing the power gay greenbacks provide in tough elections," said Vic Basile, the executive director of the fund. "Not long ago there was the fear it would be a liability. Now they are more likely to call a press conference." In the first few years after Stonewall, "politically, we were whipping boys," said Martin Algaze, a former aide to Assemblyman Jerrold Nadler, a Manhattan Democrat.

"Now we are so powerful politically," Mr. Algaze said. "Everybody takes us seriously now, they may not like us, but they know we fight back."

In New York, Ms. Apuzzo moderated a mayoral candidates' night last month at the Lesbian and Gay Community Services Center. Four candidates appeared — Mayor Koch; Richard Ravitch, the former chairman of the Metropolitan Transportation Authority; David N. Dinkins, the Manhattan Borough President, and Harrison J. Goldin, the City Comptroller.

As she faced the audience of 400 people last month, Ms. Apuzzo thought about how different the forum was from its beginnings 12 years ago, when over a period of several weeks, the candidates met with a small group of lesbians and gay men, not in a public place, but in a penthouse apartment. Some of the people who were there, she recalled, "didn't use their last names and wouldn't appear at a press conference when we announced who we were supporting."

One generation witnessed Stonewall. Now it is 20 years later and some homosexuals say Stonewall's most enduring legacy will be felt by the next generation. Donna Lee, a 16-year-old sophomore at the Harvey Milk School shares that view. She said she thinks homosexuals will face less discrimination during her lifetime than they have in the past.

"Now we don't have undercover cops coming into our clubs and arresting us, and that's very good," she said. "I feel like I can walk down the street holding my lover's hand."

For Young Gays on the Streets, Survival Comes Before Pride; Few Beds for Growing Class of Homeless

BY ANDREW JACOBS | JUNE 27, 2004

DAVID ANTOINE'S coming out last year did not exactly fill his family with pride. A few months shy of his high school graduation, Mr. Antoine said, his mother told him to pack his bags, and he was suddenly out on the icy streets of Brooklyn, his life stuffed into a trash bag, his bed the hard back of a subway car rumbling from one end of the city to the other.

Brian Murray is still trying to find his place in what is known as the gay community. A good night is the soft bed of a stranger and $100 in the morning. A bad night is an empty stomach, a park bench and the rousing jolt of a nightstick on his bare feet as he is ordered to move on.

Like Mr. Antoine and Mr. Murray, his friends, Michael Leatherbury, 25, would consider cheering his gay brothers and sisters marching down Fifth Avenue this afternoon if he had a few coins in his pocket and a place to call his own. No sense flirting with strangers, he says, when home is a lumpy cot in a city shelter. "Being homeless is not exactly conducive to dating," he says with a shrug. "These days, I'm not feeling very prideful."

As hundreds of thousands of people flock to New York today for the annual celebration of the 1969 Stonewall uprising and the birth of the modern gay rights movement, few are likely to give a moment's thought to their homeless brethren, a growing legion of the disowned and the dispossessed, most of them black and Latino, an increasing number of them H.I.V. positive and still in the throes of adolescence.

With just two dozen beds available for gay, lesbian and transgender youth, they endure violence in the city's shelters, camp out in doorways in Harlem or pass the night at a 24-hour Internet cafe next to

Disney's New Amsterdam Theater on 42nd Street. There, many of them trawl the Web for paying "dates" or try their luck on Christopher Street in the far West Village, where some quick work in a passing car might yield $30. "You've got to do what you've got to do to survive," says Mr. Murray, who is 22 and has been turning tricks in the Village since he was 15.

There is no official count of those who are homeless and gay in New York, but Carl Siciliano, who runs the city's largest shelter for gay young adults, puts their numbers in the thousands. Most national studies estimate that as many as half of all homeless youth are lesbian or gay, many of them tossed out by parents who scorn homosexuality for a variety of reasons.

As director of the Ali Fourney Center in Manhattan, Mr. Siciliano can shelter only 12 people at a time and wring his hands as the waiting list grows beyond 100. He seethes with indignation when talking about the teenagers who are forced onto the streets, where they quickly become acquainted with drugs, hustling, violence and the virus that causes AIDS. For many, he says, suicide becomes the only way out.

The number of homeless teenagers is growing, Mr. Siciliano says, inadvertently fueled by the identity-affirming pitch of gay rights advocates and the feel-good wit of television shows like "Queer Eye for the Straight Guy" and "Will and Grace," which encourage adolescents to declare their sexuality to parents on the opposite side of a yawning generation gap.

"I think it's shameful that these kids are out there alone and in danger, in a city where gay men have so much money," he says.

Young black men like Mr. Antoine and Mr. Murray spend most of their time in Harlem, where they can melt into the bustle of 125th Street. Down in Greenwich Village or in Chelsea, Mr. Leatherbury says, "You feel like a foreigner, someone who doesn't belong."

When they are not looking for legitimate work, filling out applications in stores and restaurants, they cruise Marcus Garvey and

Morningside Parks, or shop their wares along a gritty stretch of Third Avenue near the Willis Avenue Bridge. It is a perilous circuit, and in recent years, three gay homeless teenagers have been killed in Harlem, their deaths still unsolved.

During the day, as many as two dozen of them gather in the offices of Gay Men of African Descent in Harlem, commonly known as GMAD, where they play video games, grab cheese sandwiches and stuff condoms into AIDS-prevention handouts. Omar-Xavior Ford, the organization's overworked youth coordinator, serves as their surrogate father, offering job advice, wrangling beds in the better shelters and trying, with mixed success, to help them steer clear of the city's perils. "The streets of New York will eventually consume them," he says. "If it doesn't kill them, there's no way to reverse the damage it's caused."

At night, when the office closes, the young men are on their own. It is the night before Gay Pride weekend, and Christopher Street is already thick with out-of-town revelers. Brian Murray rarely comes downtown anymore. He prefers to make his money on Jerome Avenue in the Bronx or at a pornographic video store near Madison Square Garden, where he can earn money satisfying customers in private video booths. "I've already come through and conquered this place," he says, voguing exuberantly as if the pavement were a fashion show runway.

With their colorful do-rags, baseball caps and barbed banter, the homeless youths easily blend in with the boisterous crowd. Most carry cellphones, but without money to buy minutes, the phones serve simply as fashion props.

Mr. Murray's friends, more recent arrivals on the scene, are not yet as jaded. This is only Robert Marable's second visit to the Village, the epicenter of gay America, and the hurly-burly is overwhelming. Mr. Marable, 19, from Brooklyn, who lived in shelters for the last three years and only recently came out of the closet, wonders why everyone is looking at him. "I'm still not used to this," he says, putting on a tough-guy grimace and shielding his eyes with a pair of blue-tinted sunglasses.

As they gather on the Christopher Street pier, the sound of traffic muffled by the water, they grow quiet and tell their stories, which vary in detail but invariably have the same ending.

Like the others, Michael Leatherbury lives in a city shelter, but he has a high school diploma, a solid résumé and a part-time job as a customer service representative for a local newspaper. Shy and introspective, he moved to New York from Philadelphia last winter with his partner, invited by a friend who offered a bed in her Bronx apartment. The woman turned out to be a mentally unstable cocaine addict, and one morning last January, she told the two of them to leave. They checked themselves into a shelter on Wards Island, and their relationship quickly folded. "We ended up taking our stress out on one another instead of comforting one another," he says.

Mr. Leatherbury's family, deeply religious and offended by his sexuality, have spurned his requests for help, and his $250 weekly paycheck covers little more than food and subway fare. Afternoons are spent looking for more work; at night, he watches his back as he walks the dodgy streets near the shelter in East Williamsburg, Brooklyn.

"Right now I'm in a depressed state," he says, staring into the blackness of the Hudson. "I feel myself slipping away more and more every day."

If Mr. Leatherbury wears his despondency on his sleeve, Mr. Murray has learned to bury his beneath a brassy, finger-snapping veneer, although rage is never far from the surface. His childhood, as he tells it, was a horrifying time of sexual abuse by an aunt, and then for a brief period, physical abuse at the hands of his alcoholic mother. "If she couldn't find the television remote because it was under a pile of clothing, she'd beat me," he says.

As a teenager, he used to escape from his group home in Westchester County and follow the Metro-North train tracks to Manhattan, a walk that could take five hours. When he was 17, social workers found him an apartment and paid his rent. He painted the walls peach and indigo, and adopted a black kitten he named Godiva.

But last year, on his 21st birthday, he "aged out" out of the foster care system. He says he thought his caseworker would find him another place to live, but instead he was driven to a Wards Island shelter, handed his bags and wished the best of luck. Since then, a string of sugar daddies have briefly taken him in, but his wild ways invariably land him back on the street. The high point in his adult life, he says, was a two-month gig working at Starbucks. The low point came a few months ago when he tested positive for H.I.V.

Last Wednesday, after tussling with shelter employees one too many times, Mr. Murray was thrown out with the T-shirt on his back, a pair of flip-flops and a photo album that holds the proof of his two joyous years of independent living. In a rare stroke of luck, Mr. Ford of GMAD found him a temporary bed at a church near the mouth of the Lincoln Tunnel. His dream is to get a job in "the entertainment business," but his realistic side tells him to look for work as a security guard.

"I'm just stuck in a rut, but as soon as I get situated, I'm going to turn my life around," he says, before heading back to the shelter.

Things have been looking up for Mr. Antoine, who turned 18 last week. For the first time in his life he has found love, another homeless fellow he met at GMAD's drop-in center. He and his boyfriend, Cedric Dunham, 22, have started sharing a tiny windowless room in a run-down hotel on East 116th Street that Mr. Antoine's mother agreed to pay for, although she refuses to let him come back home. Now that he is not on the street, he said, he is ready to finish high school. As he and Mr. Dunham walk arm and arm down Christopher Street, they grab the fliers being handed out by someone pushing the cause of gay marriage. Mr. Antoine pauses to explain how the two of them will marry, as soon as they land on their feet.

"We're going to have our wedding in Paris, next to a waterfall, with a violin playing," he says. "It's going to be a fairy tale wedding, and we're going to pay for everything ourselves."

Political Shifts on Gay Rights Lag Behind Culture

BY ADAM NAGOURNEY | JUNE 27, 2009

WASHINGTON — For 15 minutes in the Oval Office the other day, one of President Obama's top campaign lieutenants, Steve Hildebrand, told the president about the "hurt, anxiety and anger" that he and other gay supporters felt over the slow pace of the White House's engagement with gay issues.

But on Monday, 250 gay leaders are to join Mr. Obama in the East Room to commemorate publicly the 40th anniversary of the birth of the modern gay rights movement: a police raid on the Stonewall Inn, a gay bar in New York. By contrast, the first time gay leaders were invited to the White House, in March 1977, they met a midlevel aide on a Saturday when the press and President Jimmy Carter were nowhere in sight.

The conflicting signals from the White House about its commitment to gay issues reflect a broader paradox: even as cultural acceptance of homosexuality increases across the country, the politics of gay rights remains full of crosscurrents.

It is reflected in the surge of gay men and lesbians on television and in public office, and in polls measuring a steady rise in support for gay rights measures. Despite approval in California of a ballot measure banning same-sex marriage, it has been authorized in six states.

Yet if the culture is moving on, national politics is not, or at least not as rapidly. Mr. Obama has yet to fulfill a campaign promise to repeal the policy barring openly gay people from serving in the military. The prospects that Congress will ever send him a bill overturning the Defense of Marriage Act, which defines marriage as between a man and a woman, appear dim. An effort to extend hate-crime legislation to include gay victims has produced a bitter backlash in some quarters: Senator Jim DeMint, Republican of South Carolina, sent a letter to clerics in his state arguing that it would be destructive to "faith, families and freedom."

"America is changing more quickly than the government," said Linda Ketner, a gay Democrat from South Carolina who came within four percentage points of winning a Congressional seat in November. "They are lagging behind the crowd. But if I remember my poli sci from college, isn't that the way it always works?"

Some elected Democrats in Washington remain wary because they remember how conservatives used same-sex marriage and gay service in the military against them as political issues. The Obama White House in particular is reluctant to embrace gay rights issues now, officials there say, because they do not want to provide social conservatives a rallying cry while the president is trying to assemble legislative coalitions on health care and other initiatives.

Tony Perkins, the president of the Family Research Council, a group that opposes gay rights initiatives, said Mr. Obama's reluctance to push more assertively for gay rights reflected public opinion.

"He's given them a few minor concessions; they're asking for more, such as 'don't ask, don't tell' being repealed," Mr. Perkins said. "The administration is not willing to go there, and I think there's a reason for that, and that is because I think the American public isn't there."

Conservative Democrats have at best been unenthusiastic about efforts to push gay rights measures in Congress; 30 Democrats voted against a bill prohibiting discrimination based on sexual orientation that passed the House in 2007. (It died in the Senate.) And a half-dozen Democrats declined requests to discuss this issue, reflecting what aides called the complicated politics surrounding it.

Still, there are signs that the issue is not as pressing or toxic as it once was. "I don't think it's the political deal-breaker it once was," said Dave Saunders, a southern Virginia Democratic consultant who has advised Democrats running for office in conservative rural areas. "Most people out here really don't care because everybody has gay friends."

Interviews with gay leaders suggest a consensus that there has been nothing short of a cultural transformation in the space of just a few years, even if it is reflected more in the evolving culture of the country than in the body of its laws.

"The diminution of the homophobia has been as important a phenomena as anything we've seen in the last 15 years," said Representative Barney Frank, Democrat of Massachusetts, who is gay.

Democrats now control the White House and both houses of Congress for the first time since 1994, increasing the chances of legislative action. Mr. Frank said that over the next two years, he expected Congress to overturn the ban on gay service in the military, pass legislation prohibiting discrimination against hiring gay workers, and extend the hate-crime bill to crimes involving gay couples.

There is also an emerging generational divide on gay issues — younger Americans tend to have more liberal positions — that has fueled what pollsters said was a measurable liberalization in views on gay rights over the past decade.

A New York Times/CBS News poll last spring found that 57 percent of people under 40 said they supported same-sex marriage, compared with 31 percent of respondents over 40. Andy Kohut, the president of the Pew Research Center, said the generational shift was reflected in his polling, in which the number of Americans opposing gay people serving openly in the military had dropped to 32 percent now from 45 percent in 1994.

David Axelrod, a senior Obama adviser, said, "You look at polling and attitudes among younger people on these issues are startlingly different than older people."

"As generational change happens," Mr. Axelrod added, "that's going to be more and more true."

In the view of many gay leaders, the shifts in public attitude are a validation of the central political goal set by the dozens of gay liberation groups that sprouted up in cities and on college campuses in the months after the Stonewall uprising: to have gay men and lesbians who had been living in secret go public as a way of dealing with societal fear and prejudice.

But there is considerable evidence that this is still an issue that stirs political concerns. Gay leaders have increasingly complained about what they call Mr. Obama's slow pace in fulfilling promises he made during his campaign. Some boycotted a Democratic Party fundraiser recently to show their distress.

"I have been really surprised how paralyzed they seem around this," said Richard Socarides, who was an adviser to President Bill Clinton on gay issues.

Mr. Hildebrand did not respond to calls and e-mail messages asking about his encounter with Mr. Obama, which he described in a private e-mail forum for gay political leaders. (The meeting was confirmed by senior White House officials.)

Still, David Mixner, a longtime gay leader, said he was struck by how things had changed.

"Listen," Mr. Mixner said, "in 1992, what we were begging Bill Clinton about — literally — about whether he was going to say the word 'gay' in his convention speech. Even say it. We had to threaten a walk-out to get it in."

California May Require Teaching of Gay History

BY JENNIFER MEDINA | APRIL 15, 2011

LOS ANGELES — In California public schools, students are required to learn about black history and women's history. And if a bill approved by the State Senate this week becomes law, the state will become the first in the country to mandate that schools also teach gay history.

While the bill does not set specific requirements about what should be taught to students, it does say that contributions of gays and lesbians in the state and country must be included in social science instruction. So Harvey Milk, one of the first openly gay elected officials in the state, and Bayard Rustin, a civil rights activist, may take a prominent place in the state's history books.

Advocates say that teaching about gay, lesbian, bisexual and transgender people in schools would prevent bullying and shatter stereotypes that some students may harbor. They point to several students who have committed suicide after being taunted by peers for being gay. But the bill has drawn vociferous criticism from opponents who argue that when and how to talk about same-sex relationships should be left to parents.

A similar bill was approved by the Democratic-controlled Legislature in 2006, but vetoed by Gov. Arnold Schwarzenegger, who said that school curriculum should be left up to local schools. But there is a new governor now. And both supporters and opponents of the bill expect it will sail through the heavily Democratic Assembly and be signed into law by Gov. Jerry Brown, a Democrat who has been supportive of gay rights.

"It is very basic to me that people dislike and fear that with which we are less familiar," said Mark Leno, who sponsored the bill and is one of the first openly gay men elected to the State Senate. Students who come to view their fellow classmates as regular members of society, rather than misfits, will find that "their behavior changes for the better," Mr. Leno said.

Some school districts, including San Francisco and Los Angeles, have already put in place such a curriculum. But even in those more liberal areas, Mr. Leno said, students may not realize how recently gay, lesbian, bisexual and transgender individuals have been given more rights. For example, he said, many teenagers would be shocked to learn that it was just more than a decade ago when the state legally prohibited discrimination based on sexual orientation.

The increasing acceptance of gays and lesbians is precisely what bothers some of the opponents of the legislation. Craig De Luz, a conservative activist and school board member from Sacramento, said that in many communities "the issue of homosexuality is far from settled."

"There is still a big cultural discussion of: Is it something that one chooses, or is it something that someone is born with," Mr. De Luz said. "It is all part of the same agenda, which is largely about social acceptance. Now this is a way of endorsing a lifestyle that many people are morally opposed to."

Bob Huff, a Republican from San Bernardino, said he worried that the bill would water down the state curriculum and distract students from learning the basics.

"To have something this nebulous just opens it up to problems," Mr. Huff said. "At what age do you start doing this instruction? What is age appropriate and what is appropriate at all is really a question we haven't answered."

Carolyn Laub, the director of the Gay-Straight Alliance Network, who lobbied for the legislation, cited the experience of an Orange County student as an example of how the law might work. When the student learned that the civil rights protests of the 1960s would be discussed in history class, he asked the teacher to talk about the Stonewall riots.

"Suddenly students see he is part of a broader community, and they have a much better understanding of that community in the context of the rest of the world," Ms. Laub said. "It has absolutely nothing to do with sex; it's about entire communities that are left out."

A Sea Change in Less Than 50 Years as Gay Rights Gained Momentum

BY JOHN HARWOOD | MARCH 25, 2013

WASHINGTON — The struggle for African-Americans' rights, symbolized by the bloody 1965 Selma march, is as old as the nation. The effort for American women's rights began at Seneca Falls, N.Y., more than 150 years ago.

The modern fight for gay rights is, by contrast, less than a half-century old, dating from the 1969 Stonewall uprising in New York. But this week, as the Supreme Court hears two landmark cases on same-sex marriage, the speed and scope of the movement are astonishing supporters.

"We, the people, declare today that the most evident of truths — that all of us are created equal — is the star that guides us still, just as it guided our forebears through Seneca Falls, and Selma, and Stonewall," President Obama said in his Inaugural Address in January, in a moment of history for gay men and lesbians, who were included in such a speech for the first time. "Our journey is not complete until our gay brothers and sisters are treated like anyone else under the law."

The changes have been so swift that it is sometimes surprising to remember how many gay men and lesbians were until recently in the closet and how many hurdles there have been along the way. "We were all hiding," said former Representative Barney Frank, Democrat of Massachusetts, who in 1987 became the first member of Congress to voluntarily disclose his homosexuality. At the time, the public disapproval of homosexuality — so powerful that gay men and lesbians hesitated to identify themselves, much less seek political change — helped stunt the movement's emergence.

"This was a population too shy and fearful to even raise its hand, a group of people who had to start at zero in order to create their place in the nation's culture," Dudley Clendinen and Adam Nagourney wrote in "Out for Good," their 2001 history of the gay rights movement.

In the past century in American politics, the sources of that reticence were no mystery.

Judeo-Christian teachings, interpreted as condemning homosexuality, provided the backdrop for political debate in a nation more religious than others in the industrialized world. In the United States after World War II, the American Psychiatric Association lent medical and scientific credence to those views by labeling homosexuality a mental disorder.

But cultural changes unleashed in the 1960s began to erode those barriers.

Responding to the early stirrings in major cities like New York, Los Angeles and San Francisco, George McGovern became the first presidential candidate to identify himself with the movement by permitting openly gay speakers at the 1972 Democratic National Convention.

Four years later, Jimmy Carter, a Southern Baptist from Georgia, opposed discrimination against gay men and lesbians even as he marshaled support from evangelical Christians. During his presidency, Mr. Carter's public liaison, Midge Costanza, held the first formal White House meeting with gay activists.

But Mr. Carter lost in 1980 to an ascendant Republican Party that, under President Ronald Reagan, melded social and economic conservatism.

Before winning the White House, Mr. Reagan stood with gay activists in helping defeat a California ballot initiative that would have barred gay men and lesbians from teaching in public schools. During his presidency, however, Mr. Reagan kept his distance. Legislation extending civil rights protections to gay men and lesbians, introduced by liberal Democrats beginning in 1974, continued to languish in Congress.

The emergence of AIDS in the 1980s, however, lent the movement new energy and urgency. The epidemic propelled many closeted gay men and lesbians to begin identifying themselves publicly and raised the stakes for elected officials who were suddenly facing votes over the use of tax money to respond to a public health crisis.

Lawmakers aligned with gay activists began making alliances on Capitol Hill that had been impossible on more abstract issues of gay rights.

"When it was purely symbolic, I couldn't get them," Mr. Frank recalled of trying to round up supporters for gay rights. "When people's lives were at stake, I'd get, 'Oh, all right, I guess I have to vote with you.' "

Bill Clinton, the first baby boomer president, pulled the movement further into the political mainstream. He attended a high-profile gay-sponsored fund-raiser, spotlighted AIDS at his 1992 convention and promised an executive order barring discrimination against gay men and lesbians in the military.

"He brought us inside the Democratic Party," said David Mixner, an old friend of Mr. Clinton's from the opposition to the Vietnam War who became his adviser and ambassador to the gay rights movement.

But victories remained intermittent. Democrats lost a landslide midterm election in 1994, leading Mr. Clinton to strike a more conservative tone.

In 1996, he infuriated gay supporters by signing the Defense of Marriage Act, whose constitutionality is being considered this week in one of the same-sex marriage cases before the Supreme Court. The law limited the definition of marriage to unions between a man and a woman.

Mr. Clinton's stance tracked American public opinion, which continued to distinguish gay rights from other civil rights causes. In a 1996 Gallup survey, 68 percent of respondents opposed legal recognition for same-sex marriages. In early 1997, Gallup found a mirror image on interracial marriage, with 64 percent expressing approval.

Public resistance obscured quieter advances elsewhere. Labor unions had long been the movement's "strongest ally" in seeking protections for gay workers, said Gregory King, a staff member at the

American Federation of State, County and Municipal Employees. And as increasing numbers of gay employees became open about their sexuality, major corporations extended benefit programs to cover same-sex couples.

"The private sector was always ahead of the politicians," said Hilary Rosen, a Washington public relations consultant active in gay rights causes. So was popular culture, particularly television, which in recent years has presented an array of gay figures in a positive light.

Now those developments, and a rising generation of socially tolerant younger voters who do not regard same-sex marriage as controversial, have turned public opinion on its head.

In November, Gallup found that 53 percent of respondents favored legal recognition of same-sex marriages. A survey last week showed that 54 percent backed benefits for federal employees married to same-sex partners.

Such attitudes have produced a political recalibration that alters the debate, whatever the Supreme Court rules on same-sex marriage rights.

Former Secretary of State Hillary Rodham Clinton, 17 years after her husband backed the Defense of Marriage Act, recently posted a video supporting same-sex marriage. No other potential 2016 Democratic presidential rival has staked an opposing view, or is expected to. Senator Rob Portman of Ohio, a prospect for the Republican presidential ticket, announced that he supported same-sex marriage after learning that his adult son was gay.

The pace of change continues to surprise gay rights supporters.

In his youth, Mr. Frank said, he realized he was drawn personally to men and professionally to government. He assumed the former would impede the latter.

"At this point," he concluded, "I think my continued sexual attraction to men is more politically acceptable than my attraction to government."

Supreme Court Ruling Makes Same-Sex Marriage a Right Nationwide

BY ADAM LIPTAK | JUNE 26, 2015

WASHINGTON — In a long-sought victory for the gay rights movement, the Supreme Court ruled by a 5-to-4 vote on Friday that the Constitution guarantees a right to same-sex marriage.

"No longer may this liberty be denied," Justice Anthony M. Kennedy wrote for the majority in the historic decision. "No union is more profound than marriage, for it embodies the highest ideals of love, fidelity, devotion, sacrifice and family. In forming a marital union, two people become something greater than once they were."

DOUG MILLS/THE NEW YORK TIMES

Supporters of same-sex marriage Pooja Mandagere, left, and Natalie Thompson kiss outside the U.S. Supreme Court following the announcement of the ruling on the same-sex marriage case, in Washington, June 26, 2015.

Marriage is a "keystone of our social order," Justice Kennedy said, adding that the plaintiffs in the case were seeking "equal dignity in the eyes of the law."

The decision, which was the culmination of decades of litigation and activism, set off jubilation and tearful embraces across the country, the first same-sex marriages in several states, and resistance — or at least stalling — in others. It came against the backdrop of fast-moving changes in public opinion, with polls indicating that most Americans now approve of the unions.

The court's four more liberal justices joined Justice Kennedy's majority opinion. Each member of the court's conservative wing filed a separate dissent, in tones ranging from resigned dismay to bitter scorn.

In dissent, Chief Justice John G. Roberts Jr. said the Constitution had nothing to say on the subject of same-sex marriage.

"If you are among the many Americans — of whatever sexual orientation — who favor expanding same-sex marriage, by all means celebrate today's decision," Chief Justice Roberts wrote. "Celebrate the achievement of a desired goal. Celebrate the opportunity for a new expression of commitment to a partner. Celebrate the availability of new benefits. But do not celebrate the Constitution. It had nothing to do with it."

In a second dissent, Justice Antonin Scalia mocked the soaring language of Justice Kennedy, who has become the nation's most important judicial champion of gay rights.

"The opinion is couched in a style that is as pretentious as its content is egotistic," Justice Scalia wrote of his colleague's work. "Of course the opinion's showy profundities are often profoundly incoherent."

As Justice Kennedy finished announcing his opinion from the bench on Friday, several lawyers seated in the bar section of the court's gallery wiped away tears, while others grinned and exchanged embraces.

Justice John Paul Stevens, who retired in 2010, was on hand for the decision, and many of the justices' clerks took seats in the chamber, which was nearly full as the ruling was announced. The decision made same-sex marriage a reality in the 13 states that had continued to ban it.

Outside the Supreme Court, the police allowed hundreds of people waving rainbow flags and holding signs to advance onto the court plaza as those present for the decision streamed down the steps. "Love has won," the crowd chanted as courtroom witnesses threw up their arms in victory.

In remarks in the Rose Garden, President Obama welcomed the decision, saying it "affirms what millions of Americans already believe in their hearts."

"Today," he said, "we can say, in no uncertain terms, that we have made our union a little more perfect."

Justice Kennedy was the author of all three of the Supreme Court's previous gay rights landmarks. The latest decision came exactly two years after his majority opinion in United States v. Windsor, which struck down a federal law denying benefits to married same-sex couples, and exactly 12 years after his majority opinion in Lawrence v. Texas, which struck down laws making gay sex a crime.

In all of those decisions, Justice Kennedy embraced a vision of a living Constitution, one that evolves with societal changes.

"The nature of injustice is that we may not always see it in our own times," he wrote on Friday. "The generations that wrote and ratified the Bill of Rights and the Fourteenth Amendment did not presume to know the extent of freedom in all of its dimensions, and so they entrusted to future generations a charter protecting the right of all persons to enjoy liberty as we learn its meaning."

This drew a withering response from Justice Scalia, a proponent of reading the Constitution according to the original understanding of those who adopted it. His dissent was joined by Justice Clarence Thomas.

"They have discovered in the Fourteenth Amendment," Justice Scalia wrote of the majority, "a 'fundamental right' overlooked by every person alive at the time of ratification, and almost everyone else in the time since."

Alejo Jumat, left, and his husband, Christian Crowley, after the court's ruling was announced. The couple live in Washington and had biked to the Supreme Court.

"These justices know," Justice Scalia said, "that limiting marriage to one man and one woman is contrary to reason; they know that an institution as old as government itself, and accepted by every nation in history until 15 years ago, cannot possibly be supported by anything other than ignorance or bigotry."

Justice Kennedy rooted the ruling in a fundamental right to marriage. Of special importance to couples, he said, is raising children.

"Without the recognition, stability and predictability marriage offers," he wrote, "their children suffer the stigma of knowing their families are somehow lesser. They also suffer the significant material costs of being raised by unmarried parents, relegated through no fault of their own to a more difficult and uncertain family life. The marriage laws at issue here thus harm and humiliate the children of same-sex couples."

Justices Ruth Bader Ginsburg, Stephen G. Breyer, Sonia Sotomayor and Elena Kagan joined the majority opinion.

In dissent, Chief Justice Roberts said the majority opinion was "an act of will, not legal judgment."

"The court invalidates the marriage laws of more than half the states and orders the transformation of a social institution that has formed the basis of human society for millennia, for the Kalahari Bushmen and the Han Chinese, the Carthaginians and the Aztecs," he wrote. "Just who do we think we are?"

The majority and dissenting opinions took differing views about whether the decision would harm religious liberty. Justice Kennedy said the First Amendment "ensures that religious organizations and persons are given proper protection as they seek to teach the principles that are so fulfilling and so central to their lives and faiths." He said both sides should engage in "an open and searching debate."

Chief Justice Roberts responded that "people of faith can take no comfort in the treatment they receive from the majority today."

Justice Samuel A. Alito Jr., in his dissent, saw a broader threat from the majority opinion. "It will be used to vilify Americans who are unwilling to assent to the new orthodoxy," Justice Alito wrote. "In the course of its opinion, the majority compares traditional marriage laws to laws that denied equal treatment for African-Americans and women. The implications of this analogy will be exploited by those who are determined to stamp out every vestige of dissent."

Gay rights advocates had constructed a careful litigation and public relations strategy to build momentum and bring the issue to the Supreme Court when it appeared ready to rule in their favor. As in earlier civil rights cases, the court had responded cautiously and methodically, laying judicial groundwork for a transformative decision.

It waited for scores of lower courts to strike down bans on same-sex marriages before addressing the issue, and Justice Kennedy took the unusual step of listing those decisions in an appendix to his opinion.

Chief Justice Roberts said that only 11 states and the District of Columbia had embraced the right to same-sex marriage democratically, at voting booths and in legislatures. The rest of the 37 states that allow such unions did so because of court rulings. Gay rights advocates, the chief justice wrote, would have been better off with a victory achieved through the political process, particularly "when the winds of change were freshening at their backs."

In his own dissent, Justice Scalia took a similar view, saying that the majority's assertiveness represented a "threat to American democracy."

But Justice Kennedy rejected that idea. "It is of no moment whether advocates of same-sex marriage now enjoy or lack momentum in the democratic process," he wrote. "The issue before the court here is the legal question whether the Constitution protects the right of same-sex couples to marry."

Later in the opinion, Justice Kennedy answered the question. "The Constitution," he wrote, "grants them that right."

JULIE HIRSCHFELD DAVIS and **NICHOLAS FANDO**s contributed reporting.

CHAPTER 2

Transgender Stories

Even as gay and lesbian rights became more widely
accepted into mainstream culture, transgender individuals
have had a more difficult struggle to be seen. For decades,
the majority of reporting on transgender issues focused on
the macabre, on sex-change operations and trans violence. In recent years, however, the stories have shifted:
from allowing transgender students to use the restroom of
their choice to debates in the film industry about representation, the full diversity of transgender stories is beginning
to be revealed.

Surgery to Change Gender

BY STUART H. LOORY | **NOV. 27, 1966**

JOHNS HOPKINS UNIVERSITY announced last week that a team of its doctors has started a program to perform surgery regularly, though still
experimentally, to change the gender of men to women and women
to men.

The disclosure illuminated the strange world inhabited by a relatively small number of Americans who feel they are men living in the
bodies of women or women trapped in men's physiques.

The surgery at Johns Hopkins, which is only undertaken after
careful examination by a Gender Identity Committee composed of
psychiatrists and urologists as well as plastic surgeons, changes all
that.

The surgeons cannot change a person's sex. Virtually all humans
are born either as males or females — with either testes or ovaries,

with glands that produce either male or female hormones and with either a complement of male or female chromosomes — and must forever remain within their sex.

But the surgical knife can make physiological changes allowing a person to assume the opposite gender. The external male genitalia can be cut away and external female organs can be provided. This, along with lifetime treatment with female hormones, and sometimes, auxiliary surgery, can make a man look and allow him to act like a woman.

The operations converting men to women can be conducted so successfully that the individuals can carry out regular sexual relations with partners.

In fact, Dr. John E. Hoopes, chairman of the Gender Identity Committee at Johns Hopkins, said that of ten patients operated on in Baltimore both before and after the formal program was established, three have already been married and three others are engaged.

Two women who were converted to men married as well as one man converted to a woman.

THE 'TRANSSEXUAL'

In the case of women converted to men, the operations cannot be as complete since the plastic surgeons who perform the surgery have no way of creating the external genital organs that can function in sexual relations.

The individuals undergoing such surgery are known to doctors as "transsexuals." That term was coined by Dr. Harry Benjamin, a New York endocrinologist, who published a book earlier this year entitled "The Transsexual Phenomenon."

Dr. Benjamin distinguishes transsexuals from transvestites — individuals who have a compelling desire to live and dress either part-time or full-time like the opposite sex. In addition to this, transsexuals, Dr. Benjamin says, have a compelling urge to undergo surgery and make the sex change as complete as possible.

In most cases, transsexual development begins in early adolescence or even before. Often, the condition develops from the fact that one or both parents of a child desired a child of the opposite sex and raised their offspring that way.

A CASE STUDY

For example, Dr. Benjamin presents in his book a case study of K, a male transsexual who was operated on at the age of 26 and now lives "successfully" (the word used in the book) as a woman. K is one of five children and told interviewers his mother had wanted a girl. He dressed as a girl until he was eight and was otherwise brought up as a girl without objection from his father.

At 16, K read about the operation performed on Christine Jorgensen, who was changed from male to female in Copenhagen with great publicity, and decided that this type of surgery was the solution to his problems also.

He found a doctor who agreed to remove his external genitalia but K's stepfather prevailed upon the boy to defer the surgery until he was 21. Meanwhile K worked as a female impersonator and also served four years in the Army to try to make a man of himself, as he put it. The attempt failed.

After leaving the army, he underwent surgery and now lives as a woman.

Dr. Hoopes and his associates at Johns Hopkins plan to follow the subjects for several years after surgery to determine how they adjust to their new roles. At present, there is virtually no good scientific information on the subject. Dr. Hoopes estimates it will be five years before Johns Hopkins is ready to make a report.

The surgery is being conducted out of the belief that psychiatric therapy cannot help the true transsexual change his — or her — desires. And at Johns Hopkins, the committee members make a point of the fact that the transsexuals who eventually undergo surgery are perfectly normal mentally and physically except in their need for sex change.

The surgery is in a field of medicine capable of arousing great controversy — as it did during the Christine Jorgensen case in 1952 — but the prestige of Johns Hopkins and the subdued manner of Dr. Hoopes and his associates have avoided that.

In fact, a Baltimore Sun reporter last week interviewed 13 Protestant and Jewish clergymen in the Baltimore area and found no moral objection to the program. An official of the Roman Catholic archdiocese declined comment.

Transsexual Tries to Build a New Life

BY THE NEW YORK TIMES | NOV. 20, 1972

ROBERT IS A SLIGHT but well-built 26-year-old man with a deep, resonant voice and eyes that flash with intelligence. He spent more than 20 years of his life as a confused and unhappy female. Now he is trying to build a new life for himself as a male. He decided to tell his story to help those who may feel as he once did.

"Since I was 5 years old, I knew I wanted to be a boy. I liked to play ball, ride horseback and shoot rifles. I couldn't have cared less about dolls. As I got older, I had crushes on other girls all the time. But all I ever felt toward boys was jealousy.

"I had no understanding about what I was — I had never heard of transsexuals. At 15, I was thrown out of high school — they accused me of being a lesbian and gave me a medical discharge. It was then that I started wearing boys' clothes.

"At 17, as an experiment, I had sex with a man, but it didn't do anything for me, and I decided I must be homosexual, although I never really felt comfortable in a homosexual crowd. By then I had made several suicide attempts and been through three mental hospitals, but nothing changed.

"At 20, I made a protected stab at normalcy — I married a man who I knew was a homosexual. This solved problems with my family, but I was miserable. I was dressing as a female, and I couldn't stand to look at myself in the mirror. The marriage was never consummated, and after a year and, a half, we got divorced.

"Immediately, I went back to men's clothes, and I began taking hormone shots — testosterone, which I got illegally. This eased my tension somewhat, and my voice deepened.

"But I still had a problem. I wanted the sex-change surgery and I couldn't get it. I had no money and Johns Hopkins had a waiting list a mile long. I worked for a while as a male impersonator, but I wasn't earning enough to save anything.

"Although socially I was accepted as a male everywhere, I had no identification and I couldn't get a job. Finally, I got a job where they didn't care, but then they assigned me to the female locker room. The other women were not exactly happy about that.

"I started going with a girl. She encouraged me to come here [to Downstate] to see Dr. Jones, and after a week of tests I was approved for surgery — their first case.

"Now I have a new body, a new birth certificate and a draft card — one of the few Americans who's proud of it. I let my sideburns grow, but I could never wear my hair long or wear high-heeled shoes. These are things I've always associated with being feminine.

"My family has been fantastic. Everyone has accepted my surgery very well. And I can deal much better with them now.

"Physically, it's a different life. I am accepted and can function as a male in society without being stomped to death. But emotionally, there's no difference. I've always been a male, as far back as I can remember."

After Sex Change,
Teacher Is Barred From School

BY EVELYN NIEVES | SEPT. 27, 1999

BY ALL ACCOUNTS, David Warfield was an excellent teacher.

He came to Center High School in this Sacramento suburb for his first teaching job nine years ago and soon made a name for himself, developing a program for unmotivated students that became the award-winning Media Communications Academy. Students routinely called him one of the best teachers they had had or expected to have, the one most likely to be remembered as a major influence in their lives. He was awarded an $80,000 grant for his program, won the school's Stand and Deliver award for the teacher who most inspires students and received a standing ovation from the district's staff at its annual meeting last September.

Given this backdrop, when David Warfield wrote a letter to colleagues in May explaining that he was undergoing a sex change and planned to return to school as Dana Rivers, shock quickly turned to sympathy. In June, after the school board sent a letter disclosing Mr. Warfield's decision to all 1,500 families in the district, only four parents wrote back in protest.

But Dana Rivers has yet to walk through the doors of Center High. Weeks before classes started, the school board voted 3 to 2 to place her on paid administrative leave pending a formal dismissal, which is expected soon. What might have been a quiet if difficult adjustment at Center High to get to know the person some students once called Mountain Man for his love of macho sports has instead become the sole subject of board meetings and a growing, rancorous debate in this ethnically diverse, middle-class town.

At its core lies the question: Why would Dana Rivers be fired? To her supporters, the answer is obvious.

"The board members didn't want a transsexual teacher," said Ray

Bender, a board member who voted against dismissal proceedings. "They said they didn't want to create confusion for the students."

The Dana Rivers case, Mr. Bender said, has become a cause for religious conservatives assisted by the Pacific Justice Institute, a local conservative legal organization that demanded that the school board fire the teacher or face a lawsuit.

"One board member," he said, "was heard telling a parent that this is a holy issue."

But board members who voted to begin dismissal proceedings say their position has nothing to do with transsexualism, the Pacific Justice Institute or religious conservatives.

"That is the furthest thing from the truth," said Scott Rodowick, the board president. "This is about parental rights. This is about issues that the board became aware of that have nothing to do with the teacher's being transgendered. There are things I know that I would love to talk about, but I have to respect the rights of an employee. It's a personnel issue."

The majority on the board refused to discuss the case, but the members who voted for Ms. Rivers said the others wanted an excuse to fire her. They found it, the board members say, in a few parents who complained that the teacher had improperly discussed her condition, known as gender dysphoria, with their children.

"One parent stood up at a board meeting and said that her daughter was traumatized," Mr. Bender said. "But right after that, her daughter stood up and told the board that her mother was wrong."

But Donna Earnest, whose son is a junior at Center High School, said she was not the only one who believed her parental rights had been taken from her.

"My position is that this teacher acted totally unprofessionally," Ms. Earnest said. "My child was not in the class, but kids talk all over the school, and according to the kids, he said he had been sodomized as a youth and that he always felt he was a woman trapped in a man's body and that he was going to be changing into a woman in the fall. He should have gotten permission from the parents to say this."

Brad Dacus, founder of the Pacific Justice Institute, said he filed administrative complaints on behalf of more than a few parents who felt that their children had been traumatized.

"One student had to be pulled from the school," Mr. Dacus said, "and two children have had to be put in counseling."

Ms. Rivers, on the advice of the teachers union, would not discuss the details of the case. But her colleagues say that students learned of her plan when teachers read Ms. Rivers's letter to their classes. Ms. Rivers said that as rumors began circulating throughout the school and students began asking about them, she agreed to an interview with the school newspaper. The 2,600-word profile was printed the week before school ended in June.

"I didn't have to send a letter to everyone telling them what I was doing," Ms. Rivers said. "I could have just walked into school. But what confusion would that have led to?"

In a way, the debate is reminiscent of arguments about gay teachers who come out of the closet. But unlike gay men or lesbians, Ms. Rivers said, there was no way she could hide as she underwent a gender transformation. Her hair is long and auburn now, with bangs. She wears eye shadow, pink nail polish and skirts. She has trained her vocal cords to deliver a soft, feminine tenor.

"If there was a way that I could have gone on the way I was, believe me, I would have, because this is the hardest thing I have ever done," she said.

Until age 44, David Warfield had been a Navy electronics expert, a political consultant and school board member in Huntington Beach, a baseball coach and a white-water rafting instructor. Ms. Rivers says she is still proud of that resume, but is happier personally now. Like many other people with gender dysphoria, which the International Center for Gender Education describes as extreme discomfort with one's sex, Ms. Rivers said her condition led her to alcoholism, thoughts of suicide and three failed marriages.

"I've been able to lead a successful life, but personally it's been a real struggle," she said. "Since I started taking hormones last January, I've been happier because I'm getting to be who I am for the first time. I'm going to be a better teacher for it. It's not about being a transsexual; it's about not always pretending and hiding."

She stepped near the school for the first time this school year on Friday. Classes were not in session, but in an annual staff day 40 students and 200 teachers held a lunchtime rally for Ms. Rivers across the street from the school. Students chanted "Two, four, six, eight, we demand a reinstate."

Angela Duvane, 17, a senior in the Media Communications Academy, said students missed their teacher.

"In her former state as Mr. Warfield, she was awesome," Miss Duvane said. "We all love her. Even students who never had her as a teacher."

Watershed of Mourning at the Border of Gender

BY NINA SIEGAL | JULY 24, 2000

FAMILY MEMBERS KNEW the victim as Damon Lee Dyer, an ebullient aspiring fashion designer, who, as long as anyone could remember, walked a tightrope of sexual identity.

Friends knew her as Amanda Milan, a fiery prostitute who dreamed she might some day afford surgery to become a woman. The police who found her in front of the Port Authority Bus Terminal in Midtown last month identified her as Damien Dier, a 25-year-old man, wearing a dress, and fatally stabbed once in the neck.

Amanda Milan, as Damon Lee Dyer preferred to be known, might have been just another anonymous victim. But yesterday, about 300 people gathered at the Metropolitan Community Church, an inter-denominational Christian church on West 36th Street in Manhattan, to call attention to the killing, which they said was similar to many such attacks on those who cannot be easily defined by simple pronouns.

Ms. Milan died on June 20 after a confrontation with two men in front of the Port Authority terminal, the police said. Witnesses said she and a group of friends were heading home after a night out dancing and were walking toward a taxi stand at 42nd Street and Eighth Avenue. One of the men, whom the police have identified as Duayne McCuller, 20, began to make lewd remarks to the group.

According to her friends, Ms. Milan told the man that she, too, was a man and asked him whether he wanted to fight. Witnesses said he declined, and she walked away. Then, a second man, who the police have identified as Eugene Celestine, 26, handed Mr. McCuller a knife, which prosecutors said he plunged into Ms. Milan's throat.

Mr. Celestine and Mr. McCuller have been charged with murder, said Barbara Thompson, a spokeswoman for the Manhattan district attorney's office. A third man, whom she did not identify, has been charged with helping Mr. McCuller evade arrest.

The police have classified Ms. Milan's death as a homicide. But Ms. Milan's friends and family say they want it to be considered a bias crime and prosecuted with the stiffer penalties that accompany such charges.

"I think it was a hate crime, and anyone who is trying to call it anything else is simply wrong," said Diane Dyer McKee, who often took care of Ms. Milan as a child. "This guy cowardly came up behind him and slit my nephew's throat. I don't know why he did that. It was just hate."

Detective John Giammarino, a police spokesman, said, "It was from a dispute, not a bias crime." He said he could not comment further on the case.

Clarence Patton, director of community organizing for the New York City Gay and Lesbian Anti-Violence Project, which monitors attacks on homosexuals, said arrests were rarely made when transsexuals are killed. Since 1992, he said, there have been seven unsolved murders of transsexuals in New York.

Earlier this month, Gov. George E. Pataki signed a bill that imposes sterner sentences on criminals who go after their victims on the basis of race, religion, sexual orientation or age. But Mr. Patton said that because the wording was vague, the law might not apply to transsexuals and people who call themselves "transgender," an umbrella term for someone who does not identify exclusively with either sex.

"We hope to motivate people to push for an amendment to the Pataki hate crimes law, because it doesn't currently protect transgenders," said the Rev. Pat Bumgardner, the pastor at Metropolitan Community Church, who led the memorial service.

Members of her church's transgender spiritual group, Gender People, helped organize the memorial with members of about twenty other gay, lesbian and transgender groups. The ceremony was followed by a march to the site of Ms. Milan's death, about 10 blocks away, where mourners created a small shrine of flowers in her honor.

To many of those who attended, the event was a watershed moment for transsexual advocacy in New York.

"In her death, Amanda has unified the trans community," said Chelsea E. Goodwin, a chairwoman for the Metropolitan Gender Network, one of the city's oldest transgender organizations.

Ms. Milan's cousin, Tammika L. Clark, 25, reached at home in Chicago, said her family was very grateful for the support that she has received in New York. "To know that someone has been taken away because of their way of life is not going to sit well with any of us," Ms. Clark said. "He was perfectly healthy and just to be taken away like that, it was a devastating blow. It's a lot of comfort for us to know that this is not going unnoticed."

One of Ms. Milan's friends, Octavia St. Laurent, who was featured in "Paris Is Burning," a 1991 documentary about New York City drag queens, said it was Ms. Milan's bold spirit and sense of pride that encouraged many to attend.

"I've been in this community for 30 years and this is the first time I've seen any gathering of this sort for a transgender or a third sexual," she said in a eulogy that received a standing ovation. "Death will not be the last word for Amanda Milan."

Suit Over Estate Claims
a Widow Is Not a Woman

BY JODI WILGOREN | JAN. 13, 2002

J'NOEL GARDINER is hardly the first widow to be accused of marrying a man twice her age for money instead of love, with a stepson she first met at her husband's funeral trying to block her inheritance.

But Mrs. Gardiner has much more at stake than a share in a $2.5 million estate, including a 135-year-old brick home here in Kansas' oldest city. Her stepson, Joe Gardiner, hopes to nullify the 11-month marriage, claiming his father's widow is not actually a woman.

"There's not a widow alive who wouldn't fight to defend her marriage," said Mrs. Gardiner, 44, who was born male but has had a series of surgeries to make her body conform to the female identity she says she has always felt. "I am anatomically, biologically, socially and, most important, spiritually, female. I don't like other men and women defining our sex."

At its core, the unusual probate case, which the Kansas Supreme Court is expected to decide by month's end, revolves around the question of what makes a man a man and a woman a woman. It could have profound implications on the debate over same-sex marriage — which Kansas and at least 27 other states explicitly prohibit — and on the emerging issue of transsexuals' rights.

A February 2000 District Court ruling that sex is determined at birth and can never be changed was overturned in May, as an appellate panel outlined a formula for determining sex based on a mix of psychological and physiological factors. Since marriage is seen as a fundamental right, several legal experts said that if transsexuals like Mrs. Gardiner were barred from marrying men, they would probably be allowed to marry women. Indeed, after a Texas court invalidated a similar marriage in 1999, at least two male-to-female transsexuals have married women in that state.

"We're talking 'Brave New World' here," said Edward White, associate counsel of the Thomas More Center for Law and Justice, a public interest law firm that focuses on traditional values and is one of several national groups that have filed briefs on behalf of either side in the case. "If a determination is made that a transsexual can marry, the next step would be homosexual marriage and lesbian marriage."

But Jennifer Middleton of the Lambda Legal Defense and Education Fund, a gay rights group, says courts and legislatures lag behind science and society in seeing a blur between male and female. "How much of what we think of as appropriate for a woman or a man is biologically determined versus socially constructed?" she said. 'It's very difficult when the law tries to draw clear-cut lines saying that it's O.K. for a woman to do something but not a man, or vice versa."

Mrs. Gardiner was born Jay Noel Ball with what she calls a birth defect — a penis and testicles. As Jay Ball, she was married to a woman for five years, but at age 34 embarked on a transformation that included hormone therapy, a vocal-chord shave and cheek implants. After operations to create a vagina, Mr. Ball in 1994 changed his Wisconsin birth certificate to reflect a new name, J'Noel Ball, and sex, female.

In 1997, Ms. Ball, who has a Ph.D. in business from the University of Georgia, took a job at a college outside Kansas City, Mo., now called Park University. The following May, she met Marshall G. Gardiner, a former state legislator and chairman of the Kansas Democratic Party. They married four months later.

"We were soul mates," Mrs. Gardiner said of her 86-year-old husband, who died of heart failure aboard an airplane in August 1999.

Joe Gardiner, Mr. Gardiner's only child, learned of the marriage after the fact in a phone conversation. Nobody mentioned medical history.

After the funeral, Joe Gardiner discovered an incomplete prenuptial agreement and a one-sentence document signed by J'Noel Ball before the wedding that appeared to waive her rights to his father's estate. He hired a private detective, and hundreds of pages of medical records on the sex change were added to the court file.

Because Marshall Gardiner had no will, Kansas law dictates that his estate be split between wife and son. Joe Gardner's half is not in dispute.

In legal documents, Mr. Gardiner says in a footnote he is using the feminine pronoun only as a courtesy, and argues that the widow suffers from a mental disorder.

"It's an illusion, it's an image she's trying to project, but it doesn't change the laws of God," he said at the home where he and his father grew up, and where he flies a ripped Union Jack to protest "taxation without representation" on the estate.

Julie A. Greenberg, a professor at the Thomas Jefferson School of Law in San Diego whose law review article was the basis of the Kansas appellate ruling that sex was not solely determined by genetics, said that 275,000 to 2.5 million people in the United States were born with a mix of chromosomes, genitalia and hormones that made them neither clearly male nor female. She and others said there were no reliable estimates on the number of sex-reassignment surgeries.

Mrs. Gardiner refused to discuss transsexuality: "To me, it's like talking about a tonsillectomy." Talking about the litigation, she said, makes her miss him most.

"If Marshall were still alive, I wouldn't have to be explaining to another woman that I'm a woman," she said. "He would be standing here saying, 'How dare you ask my wife these questions?' "

A Quest for a Restroom That's Neither Men's Room Nor Women's Room

BY PATRICIA LEIGH BROWN | MARCH 4, 2005

SAN FRANCISCO — Political epiphanies can occur in unexpected places. For Riki Dennis, a 35-year-old humanities student who is transsexual, it was the women's room at a rest stop on Highway 101 north of Santa Barbara.

"The boyfriend hit me, even in mellow California," said Ms. Dennis, who was in the early stages of becoming female when she was assaulted by a stranger after using the women's room. "I said, 'Sir, I have no designs on your girlfriend.' I just want to use the bathroom."

Ms. Dennis, whose lowish voice is now the lone betrayal of her birth sex, is a foot soldier on a new political frontier: the campaign to establish gender-neutral bathrooms in public places. The idea is to make sure that transgender people (an umbrella term that can include transsexuals, cross-dressers and those with a fluid, androgynous identity who do not consider themselves completely male or female) can use bathrooms without fear of harassment.

Ms. Dennis is one of 250 or so members of People in Search of Safe Restrooms, a group founded here three years ago. It reflects a small but active movement, mostly on college campuses but also in a few cities, in which the bathroom, that prosaic fixture of past battles against racial segregation and for the rights of the disabled, has become an emotional and at times deeply personal symbol of a cultural and political divide.

In fact, bathrooms have become a cultural "fault line," said Mary Anne Case, a law professor at the University of Chicago, where the Queer Action Campaign for Gender-Neutral Bathrooms recently got 10 single-use restrooms on campus designated gender neutral.

"Very few spaces in our society remain divided by sex," Professor Case said. "There's marriage and there's toilets, and very little else."

To young transgender people, especially college students, the issue has particular resonance.

"Students are looking hard at the right to express their gender, a painful right of passage for every young adult," said Riki Wilchins, executive director of the Gender Public Advocacy Coalition, a nonprofit group in Washington that fights discrimination and violence based on gender stereotypes. "These kids are demanding the right to be who they are and what they are 24/7. They're tired of being harassed or hassled when they simply need to use a public facility."

And so many students — including those at Beloit College in Wisconsin, Sarah Lawrence College in Bronxville, N.Y., and the University of California, Santa Barbara — have lobbied successfully for gender-neutral bathrooms.

At the New College of California, a liberal arts college in the Mission District of San Francisco, men's and women's rooms have recently given way to "de-gendered" restrooms, devoid of urinals as well as of white stick figures with pants or a skirt. Signs on the doors proclaim the new restroom politics: "Lots of people don't fit neatly into our culture's rigid two-gender system."

At the City College of San Francisco, a community college with more than 100,000 students, about 10 percent to 12 percent of the students are gay, lesbian, bisexual or transgender. After complaints of harassment by a transgender student, campus administrators recently transformed some men's bathrooms into gender-neutral ones.

Two new satellite campuses, to open in 2007, are being planned with men's, women's and gender-neutral bathrooms on every floor of the buildings. Major new construction on the University of California, Santa Barbara, campus is also going to include gender-neutral bathrooms.

One reason the issue has significance on these campuses is that in contrast to previous generations, in which many sought to transform their birth sex through hormones or surgery, today's young transgender people are content with a more fluid identity.

"I use the male bathroom, because I live my life as a male," said Rolan Gregg, a 29-year-old student at the California College of Arts and Crafts in San Francisco, who was born female and, though he is taking hormones, does not "pass yet," as he put it. "The problem with not passing is that my risk of violence is really high. So going to the bathroom becomes really scary."

Public restroom use is governed by a legal patchwork of city and town ordinances and state laws. San Francisco is one of five cities, including New York, with regulations protecting public restroom access based on "gender identity," which refers to a person's internal sense of gender rather than their birth sex.

But in other places, restroom access based on gender identity is "an evolving area of the law," said Chris Daley, executive director of the Transgender Law Center, a San Francisco-based civil rights organization.

Here in California, where the governor, Arnold Schwarzenegger, speaks derogatorily of "girlie men," the battle over public municipal bathrooms began in San Francisco in 2001, when the city's Human Rights Commission surveyed use of the city's bathrooms after complaints by transgender people and others about harassment in public and private bathrooms. As a result of the survey, the city passed guidelines recommending gender-neutral bathrooms be an option in public places.

"In San Francisco," said Marcus Arana, the discrimination investigator for the commission, "the choice between being hassled or holding their water affects thousands of people."

Elsewhere in the Bay Area, advocates of gender-neutral bathrooms are beginning to make themselves heard. In January, they pressed the board of supervisors of Alameda County to adopt a resolution forbidding discrimination in public facilities, including restrooms, based on gender identity. Alameda County was the home of Gwen Araujo, a 17-year-old transgender high school student who was murdered in 2002.

But at the meeting, opponents to the provision focused on potential side effects of the law.

"You can be sure that stalkers and peeping Toms will take full advantage of this change," said Catherine Norman, 54, a substitute teacher from Fremont. She added, "Bathrooms are about biology, not perceived gender."

Whenever he is in an airport, Shana Agid, a 30-year-old transgender art student, finds himself praying he can hold out until he gets on the airplane.

"Day after day, it gets a little old," he said of a ritual he confronts at least a half-dozen times a day. "It feels ridiculous to tell people as a grown person that you have trouble going to the bathroom."

Increasingly Visible, Transgender Americans Defy Stereotypes

OPINION | BY ERNESTO LONDOÑO | MAY 18, 2015

THE DAY SHE GOT a lucky break, the kind budding New York actors dream about, Harmony Santana was living in a Harlem shelter for homeless youth and contemplating what she stood to lose by starting to live as a woman permanently.

She was 19 then, in 2010, when a director spotted her on the street and asked her to audition for a role in "Gun Hill Road," the first film in which an openly transgender actor played a transgender character in a major role. When she accepted the part, Ms. Santana, then in the early stages of transitioning, was apprehensive about coming out so publicly.

"It was either help women like me and put awareness out there, or I could just live my life as a normal girl," she said. "I chose to make a difference."

Her breakout role became part of the recent and remarkable rise of visibility of transgender Americans, a segment of the population that has begun asserting control of its narrative after decades of being widely misunderstood and disparaged. With scores of people documenting their transitions on YouTube, popular television series depicting transgender characters with nuance and an ever growing number of ordinary Americans coming out, the community is starting to shed its stigma.

"It's gone from marginal to trendy," said Susan Stryker, an associate professor at the University of Arizona, of the study of gender identity. Earlier this year, Ms. Stryker started TSQ: Transgender Studies Quarterly, the first publication of its kind.

The road has been long and hard.

In the early 1950s, a lanky former soldier became the first American to undergo a sex change operation. After returning home from

Denmark, where her first surgeries were conducted, Christine Jorgensen achieved something remarkable that would elude transgender Americans for decades: she lived openly and proudly, managing to become a sensation rather than an outcast.

At the time, Americans were enthralled by scientific advances, and many saw her transition as a marvel. Ms. Jorgensen, who worked as an entertainer, was a thoughtful advocate for people with unconventional gender identities long before most people in the United States were willing to contemplate what she had to say.

During the remainder of the 20th century, transgender Americans remained largely invisible, broadly stigmatized as perverted and mentally ill. In 1960, Virginia Prince, a transgender woman from California, launched "Transvestia," an underground publication that catered to men who enjoyed cross-dressing. Several subscribers met at secret gatherings Ms. Prince organized, but for the most part, they kept that part of their lives a closely guarded secret.

Later that decade, as the civil rights movement and swelling opposition to the Vietnam War sparked a period of social upheaval, transgender communities began surfacing in a few big cities and began advocating for their rights. They included people who had cut ties with relatives, dipped in and out of homelessness and sometimes got by through sex work.

In 1966, transgender women in San Francisco rioted when policemen tried to kick them out of Compton's Cafeteria, an act of disobedience that was among the first in the fight for equality. A similar scene three years later at the Stonewall Inn in New York, in which transgender women played an important role, helped spark the modern gay rights movement.

Among those at Stonewall were Sylvia Rivera and Marsha P. Johnson, the founders of the Street Transvestite Action Revolutionaries in New York, a group that provided shelter and food to younger transgender youth, many of them women of color. Like most of the early activists, they were brash, but not politically connected; bold, but poor.

In 1977, Renée Richards, an eye surgeon and tennis player who had undergone a sex-change operation, waged a successful legal fight to be allowed to play at the United States Open as a woman. Her highly publicized story helped alter public perceptions and made her a major figure in the transgender community.

Transgender men were slower to gain prominence and their communities emerged separately from those of women. In 1977, Mario Martino became the first transgender man to publish an autobiography in the United States. A decade later, Lou Sullivan founded FTM International, a support group for transgender men.

Starting in the late 1990s, the Internet gave transgender Americans a way to connect, organize, commiserate and learn from one another. "It wasn't until YouTube, story after story after story after story, that I realized this is an ordinary thing people do," said Rhys Harper, a transgender man who was among the legion who have documented physical transitions online.

Mr. Harper, a photographer, started taking portraits of transgender people last year to document the diversity of the community. Soon after the first images of his project, Transcending Gender, were published online, Mr. Harper was inundated with hundreds of requests from people who wanted to be featured. "I thought people wouldn't want to be out and visible, but I found the opposite to be true," he said. The desire for greater visibility, he thinks, is partly driven by a sense that at a time when gay and lesbian Americans are on the cusp of full legal equality, transgender rights are lagging behind. "People also got tired of going through life not being their authentic selves. It's exhausting, demoralizing and hard."

After her acting debut in 2011, for which she was nominated for an Independent Spirit Award, Ms. Santana largely retreated from the public eye. She focused on her physical transition, undergoing a couple of surgeries, and on her emotional health. While she's encouraged by greater transgender visibility, Ms. Santana says she hopes her history will one day be regarded as unremarkable.

"I really want to go to an audition and for them not to even know until I'm hired that I'm transgender," she said. "Yes, I want trans rights, but do I want a trans stamp on my face? No. My goal is for people to see us how we want to be seen — how we are inside."

ERNESTO LONDOÑO joined The New York Times in 2014 as an editorial writer focusing on international affairs.

Solace and Fury as Schools React to Transgender Policy

BY JACK HEALY AND RICHARD PÉREZ-PEÑA | MAY 13, 2016

DENVER — The Obama administration's directive Friday on the use of school bathrooms and locker rooms by transgender students intensified the latest fierce battle in the nation's culture wars, with conservatives calling it an illegal overreach that will put children in danger and advocates for transgender rights hailing it as a breakthrough for civil rights.

The policy drew a swift backlash from conservative politicians, groups and parents.

In Texas, Lt. Gov. Dan Patrick appealed to local school boards and superintendents not to abide by the directive, noting that there were just a few weeks left in the school year and time over the summer to fight the policy with legislation or legal action. "We will not be blackmailed," he said.

"I believe it is the biggest issue facing families and schools in America since prayer was taken out of public schools," Mr. Patrick, a Republican, said at a news conference. "Parents are not going to send their 14-year-old daughters into the shower or bathroom with 14-year-old boys. It's not going to happen."

With a jab at another job Mr. Patrick has held, Josh Earnest, the White House press secretary, said, "I think this does underscore the risk of electing a right-wing radio host to a statewide office."

Earlier in the day, the Justice and Education Departments sent a letter to school districts saying that students must be allowed to use the facilities that match the sex they identify as, even if that conflicts with their anatomical sex. For districts that refuse to comply, the directive carries the potential threat of legal action or the withholding of federal funds.

The administration had already taken that position in scattered cases around the country — from a school district in the Chicago suburb, to a district in rural Virginia to, most prominently, this week's lawsuit challenging a North Carolina state law — but Friday's directive was the most sweeping attempt yet to impose that view, turning it into a national issue.

A recent poll found that a majority of Americans opposed laws like North Carolina's that require transgender people to use facilities that match the sex listed on their birth certificates, though the survey did not specifically ask about schools and children. Republicans were evenly split, while Democrats and independents were strongly opposed to such requirements.

The events this week demonstrate how starkly views vary by region. The Massachusetts State Senate passed a bill that would allow transgender people to use the bathrooms conforming to their gender identities.

"The new guidance from the Obama administration on transgender youth in schools reaffirms a basic human right," said Chirlane McCray, the wife of Mayor Bill DeBlasio of New York City, which already has such a policy. "No child should face humiliation and embarrassment because of their gender identity, especially during such a private moment."

In Fort Worth, a deep divide became evident after the school district adopted a similar policy, prompting impassioned speeches and demonstrations from both sides at a school board meeting.

At the same time, eight states filed a brief siding with North Carolina in its legal fight with the administration. And in Fannin County, Ga., a sparsely populated area bordering North Carolina and Tennessee, hundreds of people marched to a school board meeting to insist that the district stick to traditional, anatomical standards in defining sex.

Steve Fallin, a pastor who participated in the march, spoke of a rising anger among many Christians who feel they are not being treated with respect, a fury that intensified Friday with news of the president's directive.

"What President Obama did with this letter, he just cranked up the heat on the pot just a few degrees too high," Mr. Fallin said. "I can tell you from what I saw last night, most of rural America, particularly the South, is right ready to just boil over."

Advocates on both sides said they suspect that most school districts did not have explicit policies defining gender. There are districts that allow transgender students to use the facilities that match their identities, and districts that prohibit it, but no definitive count of either group.

Jeremy Tedesco, senior counsel at the Alliance Defending Freedom, a conservative Christian legal group, argued that the administration was distorting a 1972 law requiring equal rights for women and girls in education, known as Title IX.

"The Obama administration has absolutely no legal authority to change what a statute means, and that's what they're doing," he said. "And they have complete and utter disregard for students' privacy and safety in these intimate settings."

Tim Moore, the Republican speaker of the North Carolina House, said, "We all have to wonder what other threats to common sense norms may come before the sun sets on the Obama administration."

Despite the federal directive and a civil rights complaint by the American Civil Liberties Union, the school district in Marion County, Fla., said it would not change its bathroom policy. "It's just an overreaching federal government that didn't follow the rules," said Nancy Stacy, a board member. "They're just bullying everybody."

But transgender people and groups that advocate for them praised the administration's action on Friday as a civil rights milestone.

Capri Culpepper, a transgender high school senior in Anderson, S.C., said the guidelines offered support to students like her, who can feel isolated and ostracized. She said school officials told her last year that she had to stop using the girl's restroom because it was making people uncomfortable, and allowed her to use a staff bathroom or one in the nurse's office.

"They were segregating me into this restroom that I didn't feel like I belonged in," she said.

Defenders of traditional gender norms say that changing them threatens the safety of women, allowing men claiming to be transgender women into women's bathrooms. Transgender advocates say that fear is misplaced, and the far greater danger is to transgender people.

"When you make a transgender student use a bathroom that is separate from all the other boys and girls you send a clear signal to the student body and to teachers that that student is so different that they can be treated worse," said Michael Silverman, executive director of the Transgender Legal Defense and Education Fund.

Jabari Lyles, president of a gay community center in Baltimore and the education manager for Baltimore's chapter of the Gay, Lesbian and Straight Education Network, applauded the directive, but said it would be an uphill battle to put in place.

"Hopefully, what this doesn't do is put transgender students more in danger because the law has taken a bold step on their side," he said.

Chad Griffin, president of the Human Rights Campaign, said, "This is a truly significant moment not only for transgender young people but for all young people, sending a message that every student deserves to be treated fairly and supported by their teachers and schools."

JACK HEALY reported from Denver, and RICHARD PÉREZ-PEÑA reported from New York. Contributing reporters were CAMPBELL ROBERTSON from New Orleans, GARDINER HARRIS and JULIE HIRSCHFELD DAVIS from Washington, JESS BIDGOOD from Baltimore, IAN LOVETT from Los Angeles, DAVID MONTGOMERY from Austin, JULIE BOSMAN from Chicago, FRANCES ROBLES from Miami, ELIZABETH A. HARRIS and CHRISTINE HAUSER from New York, JASON GRANT from Newark, RUTH BASHINSKY from Long Island and MITCH SMITH from Overland Park, Kan.

Ban Was Lifted, but Transgender Recruits Still Can't Join Up

BY DAVE PHILIPPS | JULY 5, 2018

NICHOLAS BADE SHOWED UP at an Air Force recruiting office on an icy morning in January, determined to be one of the first transgender recruits to enlist in the military.

He was in top shape, and had earned two martial arts black belts. He had already aced the military aptitude test, and organized the stack of medical records required to show he was stable and healthy enough to serve. So he expected to be called for basic training in a month, maybe two at the most.

Six months later, he's still waiting. And so are nearly all other transgender recruits who have tried to join up since a federal court ordered the Trump administration not to ban them from the military.

The Obama administration announced a plan in 2016 for the armed services to begin accepting transgender recruits at the start of this year. But before the plan could take effect, President Trump abruptly reversed course, announcing on Twitter in July 2017 that the military would "no longer accept or allow transgender individuals to serve in any capacity," because the military "cannot be burdened with the tremendous medical costs and disruption that transgender in the military would entail." Military leaders were given little notice of the change, which has left a wake of controversy and confusion.

Civil rights groups immediately sued, claiming that a blanket ban was unconstitutional, and the courts blocked the new rules. Three federal judges hearing separate cases issued injunctions against the ban last fall that cleared the way — in theory at least — for transgender recruits to start enlisting on Jan. 1.

Since then, scores have applied — but it appears almost none are being accepted.

The Defense Department refused requests for statistics on transgender enlistments. But Sparta, an organization for transgender recruits, troops and veterans, says that out of its 140 members who are trying to enlist, only two have made it into the service since Jan. 1.

Others have been stymied by the Military Entrance Processing Command, which has rejected some of the applicants and kept others in limbo for months by requesting ever more detailed medical documentation. Other advocates said the Sparta members' experiences probably reflected the overall picture for transgender enlistment.

The applicants are being stalled or turned away at a time when some branches of the military face a shortage of recruits, and when recruiters have been ordered to work Saturdays to try to make up the shortfall.

"I'm now on round five of rejections," said Mr. Bade, 38, a waiter and martial arts instructor who lives in Chicago. "Each time, they say they need even more medical information. My last one was a minor document from years ago."

ALYSSA SCHUKAR FOR THE NEW YORK TIMES

Nicholas Bade, a transgender man who is trying to enlist in the Air Force, outside the recruitment office in Chicago. His application has been pending for six months.

Mr. Bade began taking hormones in 2014, and had breast-removal surgery a year later. He has had so few issues since then, he said, that he often forgets he is transgender. His ambition is to become a dog handler in the Air Force's security forces, but he is beginning to wonder if it will ever happen.

Other applicants now in limbo say their transgender status rarely hinders them in civilian life. One is a rugby coach. One is a substitute teacher. One repairs tractors and heaves bales of hay for the cattle that he and his grandmother keep on a small hillside farm in Appalachia. Another moves 200-pound tanks of carbon dioxide for a job creating special effects for Broadway shows.

Most say that military recruiters have supported their enlistment, but their applications have gotten hung up in the medical review.

"We're hesitant to speak up, because we don't want to be treated as special, but this has become a huge headache," said one 26-year-old who is trying to join the Coast Guard Reserve. He said he has spent months gathering medical notes, lab results, hormone records and doctors' credentials going back four years to support his application. He asked not to be identified for fear that any public attention would hurt his chances of acceptance.

Transgender groups like Sparta initially hailed the court injunctions last fall as victories. But their optimism has melted as months have passed with so few recruits actually being allowed to enlist. Most advocacy groups are trying to be patient, chalking the delays up to the inevitable inertia of a giant bureaucracy forced to change. But some are beginning to question whether the delays are evidence of a concerted effort to keep transgender recruits out, despite the court rulings.

"We've heard people are meeting with mystifying obstacles," said Shannon Minter, a lawyer with the National Center for Lesbian Rights, which sued the Trump administration over the ban. "We want to give the military the benefit of the doubt, but at this point so few applicants have been accepted, there is reason to be concerned that there is some passive resistance to the injunctions, and people are getting slow-walked."

Mr. Minter also worries that the military may seize on unrelated medical issues as a pretext for rejecting transgender recruits.

One applicant in Ohio spent five months submitting more and more medical records, and then was rejected in late May because of knee surgery he had as an infant. The applicant, who asked not to be named because he still hopes to join the military, said he was dumbfounded at the rejection, because he has had no issues stemming from the surgery for 25 years.

The Defense Department declined to make any officials available for interview, citing pending litigation. It refused to say how long recruits have been kept waiting or how many have been rejected on medical grounds. But it said in a written statement that it "continues to comply with the court order," and that "the time it takes to review each individual record will vary based upon the individual."

Thousands of transgender troops, who officially came out or transitioned in the military when the Obama administration decided in 2016 to lift a ban, are serving now. A RAND Corporation study in 2016 estimated their number at between 2,000 and 11,000. Many are in demanding jobs and have deployed overseas.

Leaders of the Army, Marines, Air Force, Navy and Coast Guard told Congress this spring that they have seen no issues with the transgender troops. "As long as they can meet the standard of what their particular occupation was, I think we'll move forward," Gen. Robert Neller, the commandant of the Marine Corps, said in his testimony.

But the Trump administration continues to oppose any transgender military service. Before it was blocked by the court injunctions, the administration sought not only to keep transgender troops from joining, but to discharge those already in the ranks. Defense Secretary Jim Mattis issued a memo in February saying their presence threatened to "undermine readiness, disrupt unit cohesion, and impose an unreasonable burden on the military."

Last month, the Justice Department filed a motion to overturn one of the injunctions, arguing that the panel of Defense Department experts who created the Trump administration policy had the necessary authority to ban particular categories of recruits, and that the court had "provided scant explanation for disregarding that reasoned and reasonable military assessment."

Opponents of transgender service have argued that transgender recruits could shoulder the Pentagon with huge medical costs, and could be sidelined from duty for long periods by surgical procedures.

Those eager to enlist counter that transgender people serve without problems now in police and fire departments and in federal law enforcement. For many, they say, the only continuing medical care they need are inexpensive hormone doses that they can administer themselves at home.

Regulations for transgender recruits require them to show that they have been mentally and physically stable for 18 months before enlisting; a similar standard is applied to recruits who have had other medical procedures. Applicants must also have a civilian doctor certify that their transition is complete and does not limit their ability to serve.

"I think the requirements are reasonable," said Paula Neira, who heads the Center for Transgender Health at Johns Hopkins Medicine. Ms. Neira is a former Navy officer who transitioned after she left the military in 1991; she helped write the Obama-era guidelines that were kept in place by the courts.

The long delays, she said, are less likely to be caused by an intentional and illegal effort to exclude transgender recruits than by simple bureaucratic caution over a new policy.

"There is no one doing these assessments that is an expert in transgender health, so they have to figure things out as they go along," she said. "If you are that far outside your expertise, you are going to be very conservative."

If the medical evaluations continue to drag on, she said, there could well be cause for alarm. But she urged patience.

"I know how hard it is to wait — I waited for 25 years," she said. "If it had been different, I'd still be in the Navy. But it took so long to change the regulations that the clock ran out on me."

Why Scarlett Johansson Shouldn't Play a Trans Man

OPINION | BY JENNIFER FINNEY BOYLAN | JULY 6, 2018

"IT'S EVERYTHING YOU'VE always wanted to do," read the promos for "Breakfast at Tiffany's," "And Audrey Hepburn's the one you've always wanted to do it with!"

When I think of that classic 1961 film now, I imagine Hepburn's character, Holly Golightly, swanning through Manhattan in an amazing hat. But for all its fabulous charm, "Tiffany's" can be nearly unwatchable. The problem, of course, is Mickey Rooney, who is cast as "Mr. Yunioshi." With Mr. Rooney outfitted in giant buck teeth, speaking in a mock Japanese accent — well, the racism of the yellowface is more than enough to wreck the film.

Years later its director, Blake Edwards, said, "Looking back, I wish I had never done it."

Mr. Rooney, for his part, said, "Those that didn't like it, I forgive them and God bless America, God bless the universe, God bless Japanese, Chinese, Indians, all of them and let's have peace," a statement that even now seems like a curious misunderstanding of who in this situation is most in need of forgiveness.

I thought of "Breakfast at Tiffany's" last week when it was announced that Scarlett Johansson would be playing the part of a transgender man, Dante Gill, in a new film called "Rub and Tug." There's been a heartfelt cry of protest from the trans community, a group understandably made weary by film after film about our lives without any actual trans people being involved.

The trans actress and activist Jen Richards tweeted, "Until the world stops erasing/oppressing/murdering us, trans women play trans women, trans men play trans men, nonbinary people play NB people. If your project needs a 'star' for financing, then it's simply not good enough."

People who are not transgender have been quick to shout things like, "This is why it's called 'acting!' " and to wonder what the fuss is all about. Cisgender folks who've never walked in our shoes can't believe the hubris of trans people insisting that we play ourselves in film and television roles, rather than having other people imitate us.

Megyn Kelly assembled a whole panel of people on her show on Thursday who agreed that objecting to Ms. Johansson's casting "takes away from the creativity of Hollywood." Incredibly, of the four panelists, including Ms. Kelly, not a single one was trans. Which, if you think about it, is kind of like putting together a group to talk about the #MeToo movement that consists only of men.

It's true, of course, that creativity and imagination are at the core of an actor's craft. At the same time, some kinds of casting are simply insulting and offensive, Mr. Rooney's "Mr. Yunioshi" being one painful example. The use of blackface, to say the least, is another.

Still, there was a time when I felt that getting any film about trans experience made was triumph enough, and I was willing, back then, to endure cis actors playing us. When Will Forte portrayed me on "Saturday Night Live" in 2006, my initial reaction was to be charmed; I made similar allowances, begrudgingly, in 2014 when Jeffrey Tambor was cast as a transgender woman in "Transparent."

But the days of transface are numbered. "I'd like to be the last cis man playing a transgender woman," Mr. Tambor said, when he accepted his Emmy for "Transparent" in 2016 (in a role from which he has since been fired). "It's time to hand out the keys to the kingdom and open the gates."

There are two reasons why we should open those gates. First, as Ms. Richards makes clear, there are hundreds, if not thousands, of trans actors ready to play these parts. We deserve the chance to represent our own truth.

Secondly, there's usually something slightly off when cisgender actors play us. People who aren't trans don't see it; they give each other awards and weepily hail their bravery. Jared Leto and Eddie

Redmayne were lauded for their courage in portraying trans women on film ("Dallas Buyers Club" and "The Danish Girl") — but not so much by transgender women themselves, many of whom found the performances mannered, studied and implausible.

If you haven't walked in our shoes, you wouldn't notice the difference. But we have, and we do.

Trans actors should play trans roles because we can do the best job. The freedom to live our lives out loud ought to include the chance to make art from the complex, difficult, joyful reality of our lives.

When Hollywood tells us that they love us, that we belong to them, we need to resist.

Like Holly Golightly, we need to say, once and for all, "I'll never let anyone put me in a cage."

JENNIFER FINNEY BOYLAN (@JennyBoylan), a contributing opinion writer, is a professor of English at Barnard College of Columbia University and the author of the novel "Long Black Veil."

CHAPTER 3

Queer Identities

As the battles over gender identity and sexual orientation have been fought on the pages of newspapers, argued in Congress and adjudicated in the courts, queer folks have continued to live their daily lives. Gay, lesbian and transgender are only three labels within the L.G.B.T.Q.I.A. umbrella. The articles in this section show the diversity of individual stories as various members of the community navigate their day-to-day lives, explore their sexuality and change the cultural conversation around what it means to be queer.

The Woman Homosexual: More Assertive, Less Willing to Hide

BY ENID NEMY | NOV. 17, 1969

THE YOUNG HOMOSEXUAL WOMAN, to an increasing degree, is refusing to live with the limitations and restrictions imposed by society and is showing a sense of active resentment and rebellion at a condemnation she considers unwarranted and unjust.

She considers herself part of what many refer to as the "current sexual revolution." When the necessity arises, she is now more frequently willing to risk open discrimination and prejudice — in jobs and with friends and acquaintances ("some people won't talk to us; they think it's catching.")

The new assertiveness and increasing visibility has resulted in:

• A rise in attendance at the weekly meetings of the New York chapter of the Daughters of Bilitis, a national Lesbian organization. Several years ago, 20 to 40 was considered average; today the figure ranges between 60 and 125, a threefold increase.

• Active participation in some of the newer homosexual organizations, including the Student Homophile League and the Gay Liberation Front. Although these groups are supported primarily by homosexual males, a woman is chairman of the New York University Student Homophile League and there are women executive members at Cornell University and at Columbia, where the organization was founded three years ago.

• A marked increase in the number or women picked up by New York City Police for "loitering," a charge applied "for soliciting another for the purpose of engaging in deviate sexual intercourse." Ten women were picked up under this charge in 1968 and a police spokesman estimated that the ratio of men to women was, at the time, 12 to 1. A total of 49 women and 69 men have been apprehended on the same charge in the first nine months of 1969.

HOMOSEXUAL LEAGUE HAS BEEN EXPANDING

One of the aims of the Daughters of Bilitis, founded in 1955 and named after 19th century song lyrics glorifying Lesbian love, is to explore the possibility of changing present laws. The organization, with headquarters in San Francisco, now has four official and five probationary chapters; until last year the only chapters were in San Francisco, Los Angeles and New York.

In addition to social activities, self-discussion and providing a forum for professional advice (legal and psychological), the organization is prepared to assist in what it terms "responsible" studies and research.

"We are a civil liberties organization," said Joan Kent (a pseudonym), national Vice-president, Eastern division.

It is not illegal to be a Lesbian in New York State but it is illegal to perform a Lesbian act. A Temporary State Commission on Revision of the Penal Law recommended, in November 1964, that "deviate sexual acts privately and discreetly engaged in between competent and consenting adults should no longer constitute a crime."

Decisive votes in both houses of the State Legislature rejected the proposal. Subsequent bills have gotten no further than committee, although John V. P. Lassoe Jr., one of the men who testified before the commission, said that he intended to see another bill introduced at the next session in January.

"But I don't expect it to move," he conceded. "I expect it will wither and die, but I will work for it."

RELIGIOUS GROUPS GAVE NO SUPPORT

Mr. Lassoe, who was director of Christian social relations of the Episcopal Diocese of New York at the time of his testimony, and is now an assistant to the Diocesan Bishop, the Right Rev. Horace W. B. Donegan, thought that the most significant reason for the defeat was "the absence of support from religious bodies in New York State."

"To the best of my knowledge," he said, "my department and the Department of Christian Social Relations of Protestant Council of the City of New York endorsed the proposed change ... other religious groups either opposed it, or, more commonly, remained silent."

Many Lesbians have rejected the church but almost all are encouraged by the increasing dialogue between religious leaders and homosexuals. Many theologians are inclined to agree with a statement made by Rabbi Norman Lamm, the spiritual leader of the Jewish Center in New York and professor of Jewish philosophy at Yeshiva University.

"Homosexuality between consenting adults should not be treated as a criminal offense," Rabbi Lamm said, "but to declare homosexual acts as morally neutral and at times as a good thing is scandalous." The statement, made last year and repeated recently, has been both supported and attacked by other rabbis.

Whatever the general feeling on the morals and ethics of homosexuality (a recent Louis Harris poll reported that 63 per cent of the nation believes that homosexuals are "harmful to American life"), there is apparently increasing support from public bodies for a change in the laws.

A task force of 14 experts, appointed by the National Institutes of Mental Health, last month issued a majority report (three members expressed reservations on some of the recommendations) urging states to abolish laws that make homosexual intercourse a crime for consenting adults in private. Two states have such laws. The Illinois measure was passed in 1961 and Connecticut approved one last summer, to take effect in 1971.

A recent poll conducted by Modern Medicine, a publication, reported that 67.7 per cent of the 27,741 doctors polled were in favor of allowing homosexual acts.

'SEXUAL BACKLASH' MAY BE PRODUCED

There is, on the other hand, some belief that the proliferating number of articles and reports and increased public awareness of homosexuality has produced a "sexual backlash."

"The general public assumes that to remove an inappropriate law is to vote for lawlessness," said Robert Veit Sherwin, a lawyer who specializes in domestic relations and is the author of "Sex and the Statutory Law."

Despite the increasing activities of the homosexual female, many experts in the field define her relationships as "generally more discreet" than those of the homosexual male.

"With many women, a homosexual relationship evolves or devolves into a kind of companionate pair," according to Dr. Charles W. Socarides, a medical psychoanalyst and author of "The Overt Homosexual." "They protect each other and depend on each other; there is often very little actual sexual contact."

Dr. Socarides, who has treated many homosexuals, believes that "women are much more emotionally committed; they can't have one-night stands and leave."

At the Daughters of Bilitis, the relationship between Doris and Terry, two women in their 50's who have shared a home in the suburbs for 20 years, is held up as an example of Lesbian stability. Both women are scientists by profession, but Terry now stays home and keeps house.

"We don't run around and do wild things," commented Terry, who thinks there is no doubt that the neighbors know of their relationship. "If you behave yourself, pay your bills and don't offend, the community accepts you."

There are others like Doris and Terry but, according to many Lesbians, "the male-female aping of marriage is changing."

"The majority of the young Lesbians interchange responsibilities," said Miss Kent. "Alice [her friend] and I consider ourselves involved in a commitment, not husband and wife but partners."

NOT HAVING CHILDREN IS DIFFICULT TO ACCEPT

Miss Kent, who had a heterosexual relationship (her engagement was broken because "our religious backgrounds were different and the families disapproved") before she became a Lesbian, said it took her "three or four years to adjust to the idea of not having children."

Other Lesbians went through similar periods of adjustment but some said they had no desire for children ("I like them but I wouldn't want to be a mother; I might want to be a father," said one).

A few Lesbian couples adopt children. "Of course, they don't announce what they are," Miss Kent explained.

(There is no law against the placement of a child with Lesbians but, in divorce cases, there are generalities about the moral atmosphere in the home. Most judges would not place a child in a home shared by Lesbians, according to Carl Zuckerman, lawyer for the Community Service Society, "but if there were no better alternative, the child would be placed with a homosexual parent.")

Women with children, who enter into a homosexual relationship, rarely live with their partners.

"We have our own apartments," said Justine, a tall, 28-year-old black Lesbian with a master's degree, who is having an affair with the mother of a 5-year-old child.

Although "an act of deviate sexual intercourse" was added in 1966 to New York State's divorce law, it is still rarely used as a basis for action, according to Geraldine Eiber, a lawyer who has handled several such cases. Most parties prefer to use other grounds.

Jean and Ruth, Long Island matrons, each maintain a residence, one with three children (aged 8 to 20) and the other with two (aged 10 and 12). Both women are divorced. Neither divorce was granted under the deviate law despite the fact that the homosexual propensities of one of the women was known to her husband throughout their 14-year marriage.

"I had had an affair with a girl while my fiancé was in the service," said Ruth, a pleasant-looking woman with intense brown eyes and cropped brown hair. "I married him when he returned because of pressure from my family — I loved my mother very much — and I felt, too, that with marriage would come respectability."

Ruth continued her relationship with the other woman for a year after marriage. When she broke it up, "the girl told my husband." He was "shocked and angry," but the marriage continued and she immediately began a relationship with another woman that continued for 13 years.

BOTH LEFT THEIR JOBS AND STAYED AT HOME

"We both had jobs," she recalled. "When I had a baby, I persuaded her to have children so she could stay home too. We lived within walking distance of one another."

She ended her long-time affair after meeting Jean, an encounter she described as "like the old cliché — bells started ringing."

"I felt that any time I had, I wanted to spend with her. My husband thought he would frighten me by leaving. It didn't work out that way." Ruth is comfortable in her role; Jean is not. She is in her 40's and had been married for more than 20 years, but was separated from her husband when she met Ruth. She had never had, or thought of having, a homosexual relationship.

"When I met Ruth, she was just another woman, another mother," she said. "We had lunch together occasionally and I found that I had extremely warm feelings toward her which I had never experienced before. It evolved from there."

The carefully made-up face beneath the bouffant hair looked troubled. "I have a guilt complex because I'm living a lie," she said. "I lived for a long time in an unfeeling existence and I felt there must be something more. I had affairs with men while I was married, all of them satisfactory sexually, but I was always looking for someone to care for. This came to me late in life. When I see young girls who know they are Lesbians, I'm very glad for them because they have found out in time to avoid a series of traps."

Jean is an example of what Dr. Socarides terms "the consciously motivated homosexual" — people who become homosexuals or engage in homosexual acts for many reasons — power, extra thrills and kicks and, in women, often at times, "despair, disappointment or fright."

"Women can easily regress to a mother-child relationship with another woman who will take care of them at times like first menstruation, first intercourse, a disappointing love affair or a divorce," he explained.

Dr. Socarides characterizes as "ill" the true "obligatory" homosexual who is "obliged" to carry out the homosexual act and afterwards "feels restored, the way a narcotics addict takes a shot."

"It is quite a severe illness but amenable to therapy in a great majority of cases," he said. His own estimate of the number of homosexuals in New York City is about 200,000 and "in my opinion, the percentage of females is the same as males." (To Miss Kent, the number of known or suspected Lesbians "is like the tip of the iceberg.")

Dr. Socarides, who rates the incidence of suicide and alcoholism as "high" among Lesbians, insists that "a vocal minority of society is trying to sell a bill of goods that the homosexual is normal."

"The homosexuals themselves know it is not normal," he asserted.

An opposing view is taken by Dr. Lawrence Le Shan, a research psychologist with a doctorate from the University of Chicago. He believes "it is not a disease; it is a choice and everybody should be allowed to choose."

Dr. Le Shan and his wife, Eda, also a psychologist, said that the homosexual "arouses terrible anguish and enormous psychological fear in society" but that "the goal, the hope, the dream of society is the sense of the miracle of individuality."

Mrs. Le Shan thought that the change would come through the younger generation.

"Young people make no value judgments about homosexuality," she said. "They have the attitude that there are many different ways of loving and that it's no one's business. They are a tremendously moral generation. They care only about how people feel about each other."

One area where the homosexual woman appears to have made little headway is with her parents. The umbrella of parental understanding shelters few Lesbians.

"Nothing frightens parents more than the possibility that their children might become homosexuals," one psychologist said.

"I told my two brothers that I was a Lesbian," said Audrey, a diminutive, 28-year-old-brunette. "The 21-year-old asked, 'Are you happy?' and the 18-year-old shrugged his shoulders and said, 'It's your bag.' But most parents won't believe it, won't discuss it and think it will go away."

ORGANIZATION PURPORTS DUAL EDUCATIONAL AIM

The dual purpose of the Student Homophile League is, according to Helen, one of its executives, "to educate homosexuals that they have nothing to hide and to educate heterosexuals what it means to be discriminated against for something so minor as sexual orientation."

Last May, the league held "New York's first gay mixer" dance at the Church of the Holy Apostle. Six hundred students, instructors and friends ("some of them were straight, we don't discriminate") attended.

"I knew the mixer was to be a gay dance — for homosexuals," said Rev. Robert O. Weeks, the rector, who was "very proud" of the event. "It was a real revelation to me, a very pleasant scene. There was no rowdy behavior, no bad vibrations.

Father Weeks, an Episcopalian, had three students from the General Theological Seminary attend, wearing clerical collars.

"Homosexuals should be free to have social gatherings in places other than gay bars and the church's attitude should be one of compassion in accordance with the strictures of Jesus Christ," Father Weeks said.

Father Weeks admitted that there had been some negative reactions on the part of his parishioners but he chose to make the facilities available "to show that the church cares about homosexuals as people and that it is an un-Christian idea that they be shunned."

The Daughters of Bilitis (who answer their telephone on meeting nights with "D.O.B. Can we help you?") holds meetings in unprepossessing quarters on an unprepossessing street in midtown Manhattan.

Women under 21 are not allowed to join the organization, a proviso that prompts some of the younger Lesbians to inquire "do they think you have to be 21 to be a Lesbian?"

The national membership is now about 500 but, according to Rita Laporte, the national president (who uses her real name), there are many more who are interested and come to meetings but are "afraid to get on our mailing list."

The homosexual woman can, if alone, find friends in the long, narrow red-walled room, illuminated with globe-shaped bulbs. She can also, if she is with a woman friend, reach out to touch her arm or hold her hand without exciting comment. The physical demonstrations are generally mild and infrequent.

NOT MANY IN 'DRAG' AT ONE POPULAR BAR

There is notable absence of the "drag dykes," the women who imitate men in their dress and manner, at both D.O.B. and at one of the most popular Lesbian bars, a retreat of pleated red velvet walls and crystal chandeliers.

There, its portals guarded by two men who extract a minimum $3 for two drink tickets, and who are said to look unkindly on any male patronage (male homosexuals are passively, and straight males more actively, discouraged), the girls gather, young and middle-aged, white and black, miniskirted and pants-suited.

The "femmes" (the more feminine Lesbians), and the "butches" (the more aggressive and domineering Lesbians, with both masculine and feminine characteristics), talk, drink and dance to juke box records, usually with arms around each other's waist or neck.

There are also a few "dykes," the women with masculine clothing and mannerisms, who are more easily identifiable as homosexuals but do not imitate men to the same degree as "drag dykes."

Most of the Lesbians count male homosexuals among their friends "because you can feel relaxed with them — there are no sexual tensions." A number of them said that although they preferred women, they also like men and had had heterosexual relationships. A small minority were leading a bisexual life.

Almost all of them thought that straight men were generally intrigued by Lesbians. "Straight men feel challenged by us," said one Lesbian.

Many Lesbians undergo therapy; some because they have a genuine desire to belong to a heterosexual community and others because of the pressures of society. But many resent being called "sick."

"I don't think homosexuality is an illness," said one. "If I am capable of loving someone, a woman, and I feel good, why am I sick?"

"I don't think there is anything unnatural about it," Audrey said. "I wish that someday people would consider it another form of normality. I just feel dirty when I hide.

"We all wonder why we are the way we are. Other people have the same experiences and it doesn't add up to the same total. But I can't imagine being what I'm not."

Gay Parents Ease Into Suburbia; For the First Generation, Car Pools and Soccer Games

BY DAVID W. DUNLAP | MAY 16, 1996

TABLE MANNERS ARE NOT YET a priority for Claire Ji Dougherty Covner, who is happy to lunge at a salad bowl, grab a bunch of green beans and eat them with her hands.

In some ways, Claire leads the conventional life of a 20-month-old girl in a perfectly conventional-looking house in this San Francisco suburb: two stories, Cape Cod-style, blue with white trim, arbor to one side, 10-foot camellia tree in front.

Many Saturdays, Warren Dill, 7, can be found on a soccer field in Yorktown Heights, N.Y., in northern Westchester County, with his 4-year-old brother, Graham, on the sidelines. Their father, Douglas, helps coach the team, playing that most conventional role of suburban parenthood.

So much for convention.

Claire, Warren and Graham are members of the first generation to grow up in the suburbs with openly gay parents, men and women who came of age after the Stonewall uprising and are now reaching their late 30's and early 40's, the nesting age for many.

Cities are still home to half of all homosexuals and bisexuals in the United States, but 32 percent live in the suburbs, according to a 1994 survey by Overlooked Opinions of 12,500 people who identified themselves as gay, lesbian or bisexual.

"Historically, older gays and lesbians were very quiet in the suburbs," said Jeffrey J. Vitale, president of Overlooked Opinions, a market research firm in Chicago that studies the homosexual and bisexual population. "What we're seeing is the result of younger gays and lesbians who grew up proud about who they are. As they move to the suburbs, they're taking that pride with them."

Not that it is always easy to do so. There is widespread antipathy to the notion that families can be headed by homosexuals, judging from the recent flurry of state and Federal legislation that would deny recognition to same-sex marriages should they ever be legalized in any one of the states. There are many suburbs where gay and lesbian couples would not be welcome at all.

But Dianne Dougherty, who grew up in San Francisco, and Audrey Covner, who grew up in Los Angeles, feel at home in this community of 30,000, about 40 minutes south of San Francisco, where they are raising Claire, and her baby sister, Michaela. They make their relationship known to everyone involved in their daughters' upbringing.

"As parents, we decided it's a bad message if you're closeted," said Ms. Covner, a 39-year-old lawyer. "You have to affirmatively decide, 'I'm O.K. with being out.' We make it part of our lives."

Other gay and lesbian residents are making their presence felt in Menlo Park as well. "They are active in the churches and synagogues, as well as in schools and city government," said Jan Dolan, the city manager. "I don't think they're noticed as anything other than the family down the street."

In Takoma Park, Md., a Washington suburb of 17,500 people, gay residents have held leadership posts in a number of civic organizations in the last year, said Bruce R. Williams, a member of the City Council. These include Historic Takoma, a preservation group; Friends of the Takoma Park, Md., Library, and the Takoma Foundation, which distributes grants for education and community projects.

The 1994 survey found that more gay and lesbian suburbanites share households with partners of the same sex than do city dwellers (46 percent compared with 40 percent), and they are far more likely to be homeowners (52 percent compared with 37 percent).

Their social lives have also taken suburban form. "I call them the Weber Set," said Elizabeth Birch, a child of the suburbs who is executive director of the Human Rights Campaign, a gay political organization. "They are much more apt to get together for a barbecue than a demonstration."

Yet, by making themselves known, they are bound to have a significant, if subtle, influence. "Ultimately, we are going to convince America around the dinner table, and people in the suburbs are much more apt to engage with the Jaycees, the Junior League, the Rotarians," Ms. Birch said.

It is impossible to say exactly how many suburban families are headed by lesbians and gay men. But one barometer is offered by Center Kids, a family program at the Lesbian and Gay Community Services Center in Greenwich Village. It was formed by a handful of Manhattan parents in 1988. Today, there are satellite groups in northern and central New Jersey, Long Island and Westchester County.

"The gay parenting community is getting bigger and stronger, and people are feeling safer," said Terry Boggis, director of Center Kids. "Sometimes, if there is just one other gay family in the community, it suddenly feels O.K. to be out."

The Westchester group was co-founded by Mr. Dill, a 37-year-old single father, after he and another parent met at a Center Kids event in Brooklyn and decided there ought to be something closer to home. Their group is called Loft Kids, after the name of the gay and lesbian center in White Plains, where it is based. About 40 families belong.

Mr. Dill settled in Yorktown Heights, a community of 6,300 people, more than a decade ago. He needed to be within an easy drive of Earthlight Food, a natural-food store he took over from his brother. With his partner at the time, he bought a 25-by-25-foot cottage on 18 acres, which he has since expanded into a three-bedroom house.

"I always wanted a really big wedding and kids," Mr. Dill said. A couple of parties at his house cured him of "big wedding" fever. But when a customer told him of her plans to adopt a child as a single parent, Mr. Dill said he became "phenomenally psyched" about the prospect of doing so himself. He adopted Warren in 1989 and Graham three years later, both as newborns.

At the time Warren arrived home, a neighborhood play group was forming that grew to 11 families. "They were totally welcoming," Mr. Dill said. "We rotated houses every week, my house included. I've been pretty comfortable about being gay. That, in turn, gets people comfortable talking about it."

Not that young children are the best secret-keepers, anyway. "You never know what a 5-year-old is going to say," Mr. Dill noted. "A kid can come into nursery school and say, 'Dad had a date last night with Tom.' "

Mr. Dill's openness was something of a surprise to Joanna M. Bailey, who has taught elementary school for 28 years in Yorktown Heights. She is Warren's first-grade teacher, and Mr. Dill is the first parent in her experience who has identified himself as gay. "I've been willing to be educated," Mrs. Bailey said. "There are so many kids in 'intact' families that aren't getting what they need that I have enormous respect for anyone who's really willing to work at being a parent."

Mrs. Bailey said that Mr. Dill seemed to be accepted by other parents and that Warren was adored by his peers. (He played the title role in the class play, "Bear Needs a Bed.")

Mr. Dill accompanied the class on a recent field trip and was the host of an Easter egg hunt for Loft Kids this year. He has also served on the Huntersville Neighborhood Association and is, by his reckoning, the first male member of the gardening club.

"My partner and I lived in this house and didn't really socialize," Mr. Dill said. "We kept our city friends. We didn't get to know people or develop many roots in this community. Having children is amazing. The roots keep getting deeper and deeper."

Ms. Covner began sinking roots in this suburban area 16 years ago, when she took a nursing job nearby at Stanford University Hospital. In 1981, she started law school at night at the University of Santa Clara, where she met Ms. Dougherty.

The two have been together since 1984. Ms. Covner has a private practice here and also teaches at Stanford University Law School and the University of San Francisco. Ms. Dougherty, 42, is president and chief executive of a testing laboratory for the semiconductor industry.

They bought their house in 1985. Although they did not experience outright discrimination in their search for a home, Ms. Dougherty said she felt at some open houses that "real-estate people wouldn't take us as seriously or be as attentive as they would to other families."

A few years ago, almost simultaneously, the two decided they wanted to have children. Claire was adopted in February 1995. Michaela was born to Ms. Covner last September.

On Mondays, Ms. Covner takes Claire to a preschool class at the Jewish Community Center in Palo Alto. Laura Hale, who teaches the class, said most of the other mothers are "understanding, accepting, interested and curious" about getting to know a lesbian mother.

"I haven't had anybody be offended or outraged," she said. That is not to say that Ms. Covner and Ms. Dougherty anticipate smooth sailing as the girls grow up and their classmates become more conscious of a difference in their household. "We may have to spend more money and put them in private school," Ms. Covner said. "But kids make fun of other kids wherever you go."

Recently, Ms. Dougherty was sitting in a Starbucks coffee bar with Claire when a mother from the preschool class approached after recognizing the girl. The woman asked Ms. Dougherty if she was a friend of the family.

"No, I'm Claire's other parent," Ms. Dougherty answered.

"Oh," the woman exclaimed, "I've heard a lot about you."

Such familiarity seems to sum up suburban life. "We can hardly go downtown without seeing someone we know," Ms. Dougherty said. "It's a nice feeling to know you belong."

And indeed, these gay parents share concerns of almost anyone raising children in a rather affluent suburban environment. "Kids here have a lot of things," Ms. Covner said, "and we don't want them necessarily to be like that." When they are old enough, Michaela and

Claire will be expected to put money in a "pushke," the traditional Jewish household box kept for charity.

There is time enough for that. For now, the mothers are busy adjusting to parenthood. "Car seats and strollers" is how Ms. Covner cheerily summed up her life on a recent evening. As she unloaded her dark-green station wagon, she added: "See what I've become? A Volvo mother."

Straight, Gay or Lying?
Bisexuality Revisited

BY BENEDICT CAREY | JULY 5, 2005

SOME PEOPLE ARE attracted to women; some are attracted to men. And some, if Sigmund Freud, Dr. Alfred Kinsey and millions of self-described bisexuals are to be believed, are drawn to both sexes.

But a new study casts doubt on whether true bisexuality exists, at least in men.

The study, by a team of psychologists in Chicago and Toronto, lends support to those who have long been skeptical that bisexuality is a distinct and stable sexual orientation.

People who claim bisexuality, according to these critics, are usually homosexual, but are ambivalent about their homosexuality or simply closeted. "You're either gay, straight or lying," as some gay men have put it.

In the new study, a team of psychologists directly measured genital arousal patterns in response to images of men and women. The psychologists found that men who identified themselves as bisexual were in fact exclusively aroused by either one sex or the other, usually by other men.

The study is the largest of several small reports suggesting that the estimated 1.7 percent of men who identify themselves as bisexual show physical attraction patterns that differ substantially from their professed desires.

"Research on sexual orientation has been based almost entirely on self-reports, and this is one of the few good studies using physiological measures," said Dr. Lisa Diamond, an associate professor of psychology and gender identity at the University of Utah, who was not involved in the study.

The discrepancy between what is happening in people's minds and what is going on in their bodies, she said, presents a puzzle "that the field now has to crack, and it raises this question about what we mean when we talk about desire."

"We have assumed that everyone means the same thing," she added, "but here we have evidence that that is not the case."

Several other researchers who have seen the study, scheduled to be published in the journal Psychological Science, said it would need to be repeated with larger numbers of bisexual men before clear conclusions could be drawn.

Bisexual desires are sometimes transient and they are still poorly understood. Men and women also appear to differ in the frequency of bisexual attractions. "The last thing you want," said Dr. Randall Sell, an assistant professor of clinical socio-medical sciences at Columbia University, "is for some therapists to see this study and start telling bisexual people that they're wrong, that they're really on their way to homosexuality."

He added, "We don't know nearly enough about sexual orientation and identity" to jump to these conclusions.

In the experiment, psychologists at Northwestern University and the Center for Addiction and Mental Health in Toronto used advertisements in gay and alternative newspapers to recruit 101 young adult men. Thirty-three of the men identified themselves as bisexual, 30 as straight and 38 as homosexual.

The researchers asked the men about their sexual desires and rated them on a scale from 0 to 6 on sexual orientation, with 0 to 1 indicating heterosexuality, and 5 to 6 indicating homosexuality. Bisexuality was measured by scores in the middle range.

Seated alone in a laboratory room, the men then watched a series of erotic movies, some involving only women, others involving only men.

Using a sensor to monitor sexual arousal, the researchers found what they expected: gay men showed arousal to images of men and little arousal to images of women, and heterosexual men showed arousal to women but not to men.

But the men in the study who described themselves as bisexual did not have patterns of arousal that were consistent with their stated attraction to men and to women. Instead, about three-quarters of the group had arousal patterns identical to those of gay men; the rest were indistinguishable from heterosexuals.

"Regardless of whether the men were gay, straight or bisexual, they showed about four times more arousal" to one sex or the other, said Gerulf Rieger, a graduate psychology student at Northwestern and the study's lead author.

Although about a third of the men in each group showed no significant arousal watching the movies, their lack of response did not change the overall findings, Mr. Rieger said.

Since at least the middle of the 19th century, behavioral scientists have noted bisexual attraction in men and women and debated its place in the development of sexual identity. Some experts, like Freud, concluded that humans are naturally bisexual. In his landmark sex surveys of the 1940's, Dr. Alfred Kinsey found many married, publicly heterosexual men who reported having had sex with other men.

"Males do not represent two discrete populations, heterosexual and homosexual," Dr. Kinsey wrote. "The world is not to be divided into sheep and goats."

By the 1990's, Newsweek had featured bisexuality on its cover, bisexuals had formed advocacy groups and television series like "Sex and the City" had begun exploring bisexual themes.

Yet researchers were unable to produce direct evidence of bisexual arousal patterns in men, said Dr. J. Michael Bailey, a professor of psychology at Northwestern and the new study's senior author.

A 1979 study of 30 men found that those who identified themselves as bisexuals were indistinguishable from homosexuals on measures of arousal. Studies of gay and bisexual men in the 1990's showed that the two groups reported similar numbers of male sexual partners and risky sexual encounters. And a 1994 survey by The Advocate, the gay-oriented newsmagazine, found that, before identifying themselves as gay, 40 percent of gay men had described themselves as bisexual.

"I'm not denying that bisexual behavior exists," said Dr. Bailey, "but I am saying that in men there's no hint that true bisexual arousal exists, and that for men arousal is orientation."

But other researchers — and some self-identified bisexuals — say that the technique used in the study to measure genital arousal is too crude to capture the richness — erotic sensations, affection, admiration — that constitutes sexual attraction.

Social and emotional attraction are very important elements in bisexual attraction, said Dr. Fritz Klein, a sex researcher and the author of "The Bisexual Option."

"To claim on the basis of this study that there's no such thing as male bisexuality is overstepping, it seems to me," said Dr. Gilbert Herdt, director of the National Sexuality Resource Center in San Francisco. "It may be that there is a lot less true male bisexuality than we think, but if that's true then why in the world are there so many movies, novels and TV shows that have this as a theme — is it collective fantasy, merely a projection? I don't think so."

John Campbell, 36, a Web designer in Orange County, Calif., who describes himself as bisexual, also said he was skeptical of the findings.

Mr. Campbell said he had been strongly attracted to both sexes since he was sexually aware, although all his long-term relationships had been with women. "In my case I have been accused of being heterosexual, but I also feel a need for sex with men," he said.

Mr. Campbell rated his erotic attraction to men and women as about 50-50, but his emotional attraction, he said, was 90 to 10 in favor of women. "With men I can get aroused, I just don't feel the fireworks like I do with women," he said.

About 1.5 percent of American women identify themselves bisexual. And bisexuality appears easier to demonstrate in the female sex. A study published last November by the same team of Canadian and

American researchers, for example, found that most women who said they were bisexual showed arousal to men and to women.

Although only a small number of women identify themselves as bisexual, Dr. Bailey said, bisexual arousal may for them in fact be the norm.

Researchers have little sense yet of how these differences may affect behavior, or sexual identity. In the mid-1990's, Dr. Diamond recruited a group of 90 women at gay pride parades, academic conferences on gender issues and other venues. About half of the women called themselves lesbians, a third identified as bisexual and the rest claimed no sexual orientation. In follow-up interviews over the last 10 years, Dr. Diamond has found that most of these women have had relationships both with men and women.

"Most of them seem to lean one way or the other, but that doesn't preclude them from having a relationship with the nonpreferred sex," she said. "You may be mostly interested in women but, hey, the guy who delivers the pizza is really hot, and what are you going to do?"

"There's a whole lot of movement and flexibility," Dr. Diamond added. "The fact is, we have very little research in this area, and a lot to learn."

Generation LGBTQIA

BY MICHAEL SCHULMAN | JAN. 9, 2013

STEPHEN IRA, a junior at Sarah Lawrence College, uploaded a video last March on We Happy Trans, a site that shares "positive perspectives" on being transgender.

In the breakneck six-and-a-half-minute monologue — hair tousled, sitting in a wood-paneled dorm room — Stephen exuberantly declared himself "a queer, a nerd fighter, a writer, an artist and a guy who needs a haircut," and held forth on everything from his style icons (Truman Capote and "any male-identified person who wears thigh-highs or garters") to his toy zebra.

Because Stephen, who was born Kathlyn, is the 21-year-old child of Warren Beatty and Annette Bening, the video went viral, garnering nearly half a million views. But that was not the only reason for its appeal. With its adrenalized, freewheeling eloquence, the video seemed like a battle cry for a new generation of post-gay gender activists, for whom Stephen represents a rare public face.

Armed with the millennial generation's defining traits — Web savvy, boundless confidence and social networks that extend online and off — Stephen and his peers are forging a political identity all their own, often at odds with mainstream gay culture.

If the gay-rights movement today seems to revolve around same-sex marriage, this generation is seeking something more radical: an upending of gender roles beyond the binary of male/female. The core question isn't whom they love, but who they are — that is, identity as distinct from sexual orientation.

But what to call this movement? Whereas "gay and lesbian" was once used to lump together various sexual minorities — and more recently "L.G.B.T." to include bisexual and transgender — the new vanguard wants a broader, more inclusive abbreviation. "Youth today

The University of Pennsylvania freshmen, from left, Anastasiya Kudryashova, Roderick Cook, Britt Gilbert, Kate Campbell, Gabriel Ojeda-Sague and Santiago Cortes.

do not define themselves on the spectrum of L.G.B.T.," said Shane Windmeyer, a founder of Campus Pride, a national student advocacy group based in Charlotte, N.C.

Part of the solution has been to add more letters, and in recent years the post-post-post-gay-rights banner has gotten significantly longer, some might say unwieldy. The emerging rubric is "L.G.B.T.Q.I.A.," which stands for different things, depending on whom you ask.

"Q" can mean "questioning" or "queer," an umbrella term itself, formerly derogatory before it was appropriated by gay activists in the 1990s. "I" is for "intersex," someone whose anatomy is not exclusively male or female. And "A" stands for "ally" (a friend of the cause) or "asexual," characterized by the absence of sexual attraction.

It may be a mouthful, but it's catching on, especially on liberal-arts campuses.

The University of Missouri, Kansas City, for example, has an L.G.B.T.Q.I.A. Resource Center that, among other things, helps student locate "gender-neutral" restrooms on campus. Vassar College offers an L.G.B.T.Q.I.A. Discussion Group on Thursday afternoons. Lehigh University will be hosting its second annual L.G.B.T.Q.I.A. Intercollegiate Conference next month, followed by a Queer Prom. Amherst College even has an L.G.B.T.Q.Q.I.A.A. center, where every group gets its own letter.

The term is also gaining traction on social media sites like Twitter and Tumblr, where posts tagged with "lgbtqia" suggest a younger, more progressive outlook than posts that are merely labeled "lgbt."

"There's a very different generation of people coming of age, with completely different conceptions of gender and sexuality," said Jack Halberstam (formerly Judith), a transgender professor at the University of Southern California and the author, most recently, of "Gaga Feminism: Sex, Gender, and the End of Normal."

"When you see terms like L.G.B.T.Q.I.A.," Professor Halberstam added, "it's because people are seeing all the things that fall out of the binary, and demanding that a name come into being."

And with a plethora of ever-expanding categories like "gender-queer" and "androgyne" to choose from, each with an online subculture, piecing together a gender identity can be as D.I.Y. as making a Pinterest board.

But sometimes L.G.B.T.Q.I.A. is not enough. At the University of Pennsylvania last fall, eight freshmen united in the frustration that no campus group represented them.

Sure, Penn already had some two dozen gay student groups, including Queer People of Color, Lambda Alliance and J-Bagel, which bills itself as the university's "Jewish L.G.B.T.Q.I.A. Community." But none focused on gender identity (the closest, Trans Penn, mostly catered to faculty members and graduate students).

Richard Parsons, an 18-year-old transgender male, discovered that when he attended a student mixer called the Gay Affair, sponsored by

Penn's L.G.B.T. Center. "I left thoroughly disappointed," said Richard, a garrulous freshman with close-cropped hair, wire-framed glasses and preppy clothes, who added, "This is the L.G.B.T. Center, and it's all gay guys."

Through Facebook, Richard and others started a group called Penn Non-Cis, which is short for "non-cisgender." For those not fluent in gender-studies speak, "cis" means "on the same side as" and "cisgender" denotes someone whose gender identity matches his or her biology, which describes most of the student body. The group seeks to represent everyone else. "This is a freshman uprising," Richard said.

On a brisk Tuesday night in November, about 40 students crowded into the L.G.B.T. Center, a converted 19th-century carriage house, for the group's inaugural open mike. The organizers had lured students by handing out fliers on campus while barking: "Free condoms! Free ChapStick!"

"There's a really vibrant L.G.B.T. scene," Kate Campbell, one of the M.C.'s, began. "However, that mostly encompasses the L.G.B. and not too much of the T. So we're aiming to change that."

Students read poems and diary entries, and sang guitar ballads. Then Britt Gilbert — a punky-looking freshman with a blond bob, chunky glasses and a rock band T-shirt — took the stage. She wanted to talk about the concept of "bi-gender."

"Does anyone want to share what they think it is?"

Silence.

She explained that being bi-gender is like manifesting both masculine and feminine personas, almost as if one had a "detachable penis." "Some days I wake up and think, 'Why am I in this body?' " she said. "Most days I wake up and think, 'What was I thinking yesterday?' "

Britt's grunginess belies a warm matter-of-factness, at least when describing her journey. As she elaborated afterward, she first heard the term "bi-gender" from Kate, who found it on Tumblr. The two met at freshman orientation and bonded. In high school, Kate identified as "agender" and used the singular pronoun "they"; she now sees her gender as an "amorphous blob."

By contrast, Britt's evolution was more linear. She grew up in suburban Pennsylvania and never took to gender norms. As a child, she worshiped Cher and thought boy bands were icky. Playing video games, she dreaded having to choose male or female avatars.

In middle school, she started calling herself bisexual and dated boys. By 10th grade, she had come out as a lesbian. Her parents thought it was a phase — until she brought home a girlfriend, Ash. But she still wasn't settled.

"While I definitely knew that I liked girls, I didn't know that I was one," Britt said. Sometimes she would leave the house in a dress and feel uncomfortable, as if she were wearing a Halloween costume. Other days, she felt fine. She wasn't "trapped in the wrong body," as the cliché has it — she just didn't know which body she wanted.

When Kate told her about the term "bi-gender," it clicked instantly. "I knew what it was, before I knew what it was," Britt said, adding that it is more fluid than "transgender" but less vague than "gender-queer" — a catchall term for nontraditional gender identities.

At first, the only person she told was Ash, who responded, "It took you this long to figure it out?" For others, the concept was not so easy to grasp. Coming out as a lesbian had been relatively simple, Britt said, "since people know what that is." But when she got to Penn, she was relieved to find a small community of freshmen who had gone through similar awakenings.

Among them was Richard Parsons, the group's most politically lucid member. Raised female, Richard grew up in Orlando, Fla., and realized he was transgender in high school. One summer, he wanted to room with a transgender friend at camp, but his mother objected. "She's like, 'Well, if you say that he's a guy, then I don't want you rooming with a guy,' " he recalled. "We were in a car and I basically blurted out, 'I think I might be a guy, too!' "

After much door-slamming and tears, Richard and his mother

reconciled. But when she asked what to call him, he had no idea. He chose "Richard" on a whim, and later added a middle name, Matthew, because it means "gift of God."

By the time he got to Penn, he had been binding his breasts for more than two years and had developed back pain. At the open mike, he told a harrowing story about visiting the university health center for numbness and having a panic attack when he was escorted into a women's changing room.

Nevertheless, he praised the university for offering gender-neutral housing. The college's medical program also covers sexual reassignment surgery, which, he added, "has heavily influenced my decision to probably go under the Penn insurance plan next year."

Penn has not always been so forward-thinking; a decade ago, the L.G.B.T. Center (nestled amid fraternity houses) was barely used. But in 2010, the university began reaching out to applicants whose essays raised gay themes. Last year, the gay newsmagazine The Advocate ranked Penn among the top 10 trans-friendly universities, alongside liberal standbys like New York University.

More and more colleges, mostly in the Northeast, are catering to gender-nonconforming students. According to a survey by Campus Pride, at least 203 campuses now allow transgender students to room with their preferred gender; 49 have a process to change one's name and gender in university records; and 57 cover hormone therapy. In December, the University of Iowa became the first to add a "transgender" checkbox to its college application.

"I wrote about an experience I had with a drag queen as my application essay for all the Ivy Leagues I applied to," said Santiago Cortes, one of the Penn students. "And I got into a few of the Ivy Leagues — Dartmouth, Columbia and Penn. Strangely not Brown."

But even these measures cannot keep pace with the demands of incoming students, who are challenging the curriculum much as gay activists did in the '80s and '90s. Rather than protest the lack of gay studies classes, they are critiquing existing ones for being too narrow.

Several members of Penn Non-Cis had been complaining among themselves about a writing seminar they were taking called "Beyond 'Will & Grace,'" which examined gay characters on shows like "Ellen," "Glee" and "Modern Family." The professor, Gail Shister, who is a lesbian, had criticized several students for using "L.G.B.T.Q." in their essays, saying it was clunky, and proposed using "queer" instead. Some students found the suggestion offensive, including Britt Gilbert, who described Ms. Shister as "unaccepting of things that she doesn't understand."

Ms. Shister, reached by phone, said the criticism was strictly grammatical. "I am all about economy of expression," she said. "L.G.B.T.Q. doesn't exactly flow off the tongue. So I tell the students, 'Don't put in an acronym with five or six letters.'"

One thing is clear. Ms. Shister, who is 60 and in 1979 became The Philadelphia Inquirer's first female sportswriter, is of a different generation, a fact she acknowledges freely, even gratefully. "Frankly, I'm both proud and envious that these young people are growing up in an age where they're free to love who they want," she said.

If history is any guide, the age gap won't be so easy to overcome. As liberated gay men in the 1970s once baffled their pre-Stonewall forebears, the new gender outlaws, to borrow a phrase from the transgender writer Kate Bornstein, may soon be running ideological circles around their elders.

Still, the alphabet soup of L.G.B.T.Q.I.A. may be difficult to sustain. "In the next 10 or 20 years, the various categories heaped under the umbrella of L.G.B.T. will become quite quotidian," Professor Halberstam said.

Even at the open mike, as students picked at potato chips and pineapple slices, the bounds of identity politics were spilling over and becoming blurry.

At one point, Santiago, a curly-haired freshman from Colombia, stood before the crowd. He and a friend had been pondering the limits of what he calls "L.G.B.T.Q. plus."

"Why do only certain letters get to be in the full acronym?" he asked.

Then he rattled off a list of gender identities, many culled from Wikipedia. "We have our lesbians, our gays," he said, before adding, "bisexual, transsexual, queer, homosexual, asexual." He took a breath and continued. "Pansexual. Omnisexual. Trisexual. Agender. Bi-gender. Third gender. Transgender. Transvestite. Intersexual. Two-spirit. Hijra. Polyamorous."

By now, the list had turned into free verse. He ended: "Undecided. Questioning. Other. Human."

The room burst into applause.

If You're Asking, 'Am I Gay? Lesbian? Bi? Trans? Queer?' Here's a Start

BY MAYA SALAM | MAY 17, 2017

MAYBE THE QUESTIONS bubbled up over time. Maybe the realization hit you suddenly. Am I gay? Everyone calls me a girl, but I don't feel like one. Why do I feel different from the people I'm around? Those feelings can be the beginning of a journey of self-discovery that can be rewarding, but also extremely daunting.

'YOU ARE NOT ALONE.'

If this is what you're going through, take a breath and remember that there are plenty of people and resources to help and support you. Even if facing discrimination is not a concern for you, the anxiety and isolation you may feel privately can be all too real.

"You are not alone," said iO Tillett Wright, a speaker whose Tedx-Women talk, "Fifty Shades of Gay," has more than 2.5 million views. "It's comical how not alone you are."

While it is not possible to get an exact figure on the population of lesbian, gay, bisexual and transgender Americans, a 2015 report by the Public Religion Research Institute suggests that "7 percent of millennials identify either as lesbian, gay, bisexual or transgender." A January 2017 Gallup survey revealed that an estimated 4.1 percent of Americans identify as lesbian, gay, bisexual or transgender, up from 3.5 percent in 2012.

According to a paper published by the National Bureau of Economic Research, even those numbers may be underestimated — as are the challenges that people in this community face.

In many parts of the country, and the world, there are institutional resources available for lesbian, gay, bisexual, transgender and queer people that never before existed, said Larry Gross, a communications professor at the University of Southern California who helped found the field of gay and lesbian studies.

"And rather importantly," he added, "psychological, psychiatric, medical professionals are now much more aware and enlightened than they were in the past not to pathologize variation, but to see it as normal, and to help people to adjust."

At square one, though, take an inventory of your feelings.

YOU DON'T NEED ALL THE ANSWERS RIGHT AWAY.

"The leap from 'something feels not right' to 'I am transgender' is a huge one," said Mr. Tillett Wright, whose Self Evident Truths project is documenting 10,000 people who identify as anything other than 100 percent straight. "I think that the pervasive idea is that there's this switch that you flip that's like, 'I'm not straight anymore, I'm gay,' or 'Something's up, and I'm trans.' "

"The big question is: 'Am I happy?'," he said. "Do I feel good? Do I feel at ease?"

Richard H. Reams, the associate director of counseling services at Trinity University, in San Antonio, Tex., who created the guide "Am I Gay?" recommends that those questioning their orientation should also assess whether their same-sex attractions are physical or emotional.

Physical attraction toward someone of the same sex can be easier to identify, Dr. Reams said, indicated by thoughts as simple as, "I'd like to touch that person."

Emotional attraction can be trickier: "What are my feelings toward the different people in my life? Is it just friendship feelings, or is it romantic feelings?" Dr. Reams suggests asking yourself. And don't rush answering.

If negative thoughts like "something is wrong with me" creep up, Deborah Coolhart, a therapist at Syracuse University and co-author of "The Gender Quest Workbook," says to remember that these thoughts are learned, not innate. She works with patients to help them identify the origin of those critical messages to hopefully "externalize them," she said.

DISPEL THE MYTHS.

Among the most damaging myths are that being a sexual minority or transgender is a disease, a sin or not normal, says Dr. Coolhart, who specializes in transgender issues. All of these thoughts need to be challenged, she said.

By connecting with affirmative people, like counselors and other helping professionals, or a community, those messages can be replaced with: " 'I am normal. There's a lot of people that have this experience. There's nothing wrong with me. This is actually something that makes me special and who I am,' " she said.

Dr. Reams addresses several myths about sexual orientation on his website but says the most common one is that bisexuals are equally attracted to men and woman. "It infuriates me," he said. "Bisexuality is a spectrum."

The traditional definition of sexual orientation assumes two primary things, he says: that people have a gender identity of male or female, and that they're attracted to men, women or both. "Both of those assumptions can be incorrect," he said. In fact, genderqueer or gender-fluid individuals may have an unfixed gender identity.

If Mr. Tillett Wright, who is transgender, could give advice to his younger self, it would be to waste less time trying to be "straight and femme."

"You can never bend yourself into being anything other than what you are. No matter how much social pressure is put on you," he said.

EMBRACE THE SPECTRUM.

Fluidity is quickly becoming a new, and acceptable, normal in the queer community.

"The old-school answer was that you really needed to come to an identity and claim it," Dr. Reams said. "We're now understanding that's not the case."

Embracing that fluidity is more about characteristics that aren't gender-specific. It's "incredibly liberating" for some sexual minorities to describe themselves beyond the three labels of lesbian, gay or bisexual, he said.

When seeking a partner, "male or female is pretty immaterial" to a lot of younger people, he said.

Mr. Tillett Wright says the healthiest way to come to an identity is to "come to it in time" and "never settle on anything."

"I find rigidity in any identity, be it straight, gay, trans, bisexual or whatever. When you settle on one thing, you have formed a barrier for yourself and your future selves, plural."

YOUR SAFETY IS PARAMOUNT.

While many L.G.B.T.Q. people live openly all over the United States, and in many other countries, it's important to take stock of your personal situation to ensure that you're not compromising your safety. According to data compiled by the Federal Bureau of Investigation that was analyzed last year, L.G.B.T.Q. Americans are more likely to be targets of hate crimes than any other minority group.

Similarly, a nationwide study by the Centers of Disease Control and Prevention released in 2016 revealed that high school students identifying as gay, lesbian or bisexual are still at much greater risk of bullying, depression and violence than their peers who identify as straight. And in many other parts of the world, people still face persecution and punishment for their orientation and identity.

So in some cases, Dr. Coolhart says, it may be better to wait to come out to everyone and to instead focus on finding support. "Think about what kind of risks there are in coming out, how supportive they think their family will be, how will it be treated in the work or school environment," she said.

To start, Dr. Coolhart suggests, find one person you can be honest with — maybe a relative, teacher, counselor, co-worker or church person.

FIND A SUPPORT NETWORK.

Dr. Reams recommends that if you can't find someone trustworthy or you live in an area that feels unsafe, make contact with the nearest Metropolitan Community Church. The church operates nationwide, even in rural areas. "Even if you're not religious, the pastor of that church is going to know what resources there are," he said. Also consider contacting a PFLAG chapter in your area or a GSA chapter in your school, if there is one.

The LGBT National Help Center offers book suggestions, hotlines and online chat services.

GLAAD and the It Gets Better Project offer communities and information. The Trevor Project is a national support network for young people, focused largely on suicide prevention, but it also extends an online community to connect with privately, and a hotline if you need to talk.

The Trans Lifeline operates hotlines for people struggling with their gender identity, and the World Professional Association for Transgender Health offers many resources for transgender individuals. The Bisexual Resource Center hosts events, offers resources and raises awareness about bisexuality.

Finding support online easily defuses a common first reaction of people questioning their orientation or identity — thoughts like "there's something here that no one has ever experienced, and there's no one like them, and there's no one to talk to," said Mr. Gross, who wrote "Contested Closets: The Politics and Ethics of Outing."

Mr. Gross, Dr. Reams and Dr. Coolhart all suggest watching You-Tube testimonials. They "give faces to experiences that are similar," Dr. Coolhart said. But skip the comments, Dr. Reams says.

Online resources like that have changed everything. "In a culture saturated in sexual imagery," Mr. Gross said, queer people can finally see themselves reflected in ways that were not available before. "The internet has overcome that kind of isolation in a way that nothing has previously."

Mr. Tillett Wright offers a word of warning, though: Exercise restraint when sharing emotional details online.

"Social media opens the doors to keyboard warriors, who like to bully people," he said. "So as you're tiptoeing your way into your identity and figuring yourself out, maybe don't put your most vulnerable stuff out there for everybody to pick apart."

Online or off, Dr. Reams said, it is most important to find someone to talk to who is supportive and nonjudgmental. "That is the most wonderful thing that a person can have."

When Everyone Can
Be 'Queer,' Is Anyone?

BY JENNA WORTHAM | JULY 12, 2016

EARLIER THIS YEAR, Vice published an essay that posed the question "Can Straight People Be Queer?" The article includes an image from Jaden Smith's Facebook page of the musician looking petulant in a skirt, alongside the caption "My mood when they try to hate." It also makes reference to the model Lily Rose Depp, who once compared sexuality to dietary habits: "You could think peanut butter is your favorite food for, 5,000 years and then be like, 'I actually like burgers better,' you know?" Vice, unsurprisingly, never settled on an answer, but a reader captured the article's sentiment in a succinct and sarcastic comment, writing, "Queer is SO HOT right now."

The speed with which modern society has adapted to accommodate the world's vast spectrum of gender and sexual identities may be the most important cultural metamorphosis of our time. Facebook, which can be seen as a kind of social census, now offers nearly 60 different gender options, including "questioning" and "bigender" — or no gender at all. In a new commercial for Calvin Klein, Young Thug, a slender rapper prone to wearing dresses, states that he feels "there's no such thing as gender." The Oxford English Dictionary recently added Mx, a neutral replacement for titles like Mr. and Mrs. The video game "The Sims" has even begun allowing players to create same-sex relationships and lifted gender restrictions on characters' clothing and hairstyles. Plainly, we are in the midst of a profoundly exhilarating revolution. And "queer" has come to serve as a linguistic catchall for this broadening spectrum of identities, so much so that people who consider themselves straight, but reject heteronormativity, might even call themselves queer. But when everyone can be queer, is anyone?

The word "queer" has always contained the shimmer of multitudes; even etymologists can't settle on one origin story. One popular theory is that it descends from quer, an old German word meaning oblique — neither parallel nor at a right angle, but in between. From birth, queer has resisted straightness. By the 1800s, this inscrutability had taken on a negative cast in English usage, and queer marked something as dubious or unseemly: "Queering the pitch" meant to spoil something — a business transaction, say; being on "queer street" meant financial ruin. Eventually, the word came to apply to people with ambiguous peculiarities. A "queer fellow," in 19th-century English, is decidedly odd, as is someone who is "queer in the head."

The word became linked to sexual behavior in the early 1900s, as a derogatory term for men deemed effeminate and others who upended traditional gender roles and appearances. As homosexuality was classified as a mental illness and made punishable by law, the word snowballed into a full-blown slur, heard everywhere from the playground ("smear the queer") to intellectual duels (William F. Buckley Jr. to Gore Vidal: "Now listen, you queer").

This halo of negativity began to dim somewhat in the 1970s, when the word was reclaimed by activists and academics. Not only did its deliberate looseness make it a welcome alternative to the rigidity of "gay" and "lesbian," it also turned the alienating force of the slur into a point of pride. (Though it is still considered offensive by some.) A manifesto distributed at New York City's Pride parade in 1990 by Queer Nation, a prominent and controversial gay-rights group, put it this way: "When a lot of lesbians and gay men wake up in the morning, we feel angry and disgusted, not gay. So we've chosen to call ourselves queer. Using 'queer' is a way of reminding us how we are perceived by the rest of the world." It was a radical word for a radical time. Protesters and advocacy groups — particularly communities of color — took it up to gather support for the fight against the AIDS crisis and for gay rights. "We're here, we're queer, get used to it" became a popular chant.

Academics saw queerness as possessing revolutionary potential. Eve Sedgwick, a professor at Duke who is considered one of the founders of queer theory, described queerness as an "open mesh of possibilities." David Halperin, a founder of an academic journal on queer studies, describes queerness as a practice, one that is an "exhilarating personal experiment, performed on ourselves by ourselves." Writing in 1995, Halperin bemoaned the dilution of what he felt was a subversive word. "There is now a right way to be queer ... to invert the norms of straight society," he scoffed, referring to clothes, haircuts, piercings, even diets tailored to gay and lesbian buyers. "How can queer modes of consumption count as resistant cultural practices?" Eight years later, the hit makeover show "Queer Eye for the Straight Guy" debuted on Bravo, literalizing Halperin's concerns. Each episode culminated in a lavish shopping trip that distilled gay culture down to clothes and hair products — and it was all done in the service of straight men.

Increased acceptance of queerness has only led to increased commodification. Every June, the month of most gay-pride celebrations, companies like Netflix, McDonald's, Apple, Salesforce and Walmart spend tremendous amounts of money to include their branded floats in the parades. This year, Andrew Jolivétte, a professor at San Francisco State University, told The Guardian that the city's event was no longer a symbol of progress. Instead, he said, it felt like a prolonged commercial: "Gay Inc." In the same article, Isa Noyola, a transgender Latina activist in San Francisco, remarked on the paradox that the same companies championing gay rights have contributed to the gentrification that has made the Castro one of the most expensive neighborhoods in the country. "It's ironic to walk alongside tech companies that have displaced us," she said.

The radical power of "queer" always came from its inclusivity. But that inclusivity offers a false promise of equality that does not translate to the lived reality of most queer people. Anti-trans bathroom laws and the shooting at Pulse, the gay nightclub in Orlando, are the latest reminders that equality has yet to arrive. Seen this way, such a sunny outlook can, in fact, be counterproductive. DarkMatter, a South Asian trans performance-art duo, highlights this observation — the way visibility and acceptance can actually lead to erasure — in their works. In one, called "Rainbows Are Just Refracted White Light," they intone, "Rainbows are just a trick of light, they make us forget the storm is still happening."

Maybe we are relying on a single word, a single idea, a single identity, to do too much. After all, "queer" never belonged to us; it was foisted upon us, and we reconfigured it to make it ours. The future will bring new possibilities and ideas — and new terms for them. Scientists are still learning about the vast and complex components that interact to create human sexuality. An article in Nature from 2015 delved into the latest research on sex and gender among mice. Sex determination is thought to happen in the womb, but studies of mice suggest that sex can fluctuate between male and female throughout life. Someday, maybe we'll recognize that queer is actually the norm, and the notion of static sexual identities will be seen as austere and reductive.

To the queer theorist José Esteban Muñoz, queerness was not a label people could claim but a complete reimagining of how people could be. "We may never touch queerness," he wrote, in his 2009 book, "Cruising Utopia." "But we can feel it as the warm illumination of a horizon imbued with potentiality." The widespread acceptance and even appropriation of the word "queer" seem to move us both closer to and further from such a future. But the horizon is out there, and you can see it if you squint.

Germany Must Allow Third Gender Category, Court Rules

BY MELISSA EDDY AND JESSICA BENNETT | NOV. 8, 2017

BERLIN — Germany must create a third gender category for people who do not identify as either male or female or were born with ambiguous sexual traits, the country's constitutional court ruled on Wednesday, finding that binary gender designations violated the right to privacy.

In 2013, Germany became the first European country to allow parents to register newborns as neither female nor male, if the child was born with characteristics of both sexes.

The new decision, by the Federal Constitutional Court, goes further, giving lawmakers until the end of 2018 to either allow the introduction of a third gender category or dispense with gender altogether in public documents.

The ruling arrives as society, medicine and law increasingly recognize the ways in which gender is socially constructed and not necessarily fixed or stable.

According to Lambda Legal, an American organization that works for the rights of lesbians, gay men, bisexuals, and transgender people, at least eight countries — Australia, Bangladesh, Germany, India, Malta, Nepal, New Zealand and Pakistan — recognize more than two genders on passports or national ID cards.

Thailand recognizes a third gender in its Constitution but has not yet made that an option on government documents.

In June, for the first time in Canada, a newborn was issued a health document without a gender: a health card that listed U as the gender, for unspecified or unknown. In August, Canada began issuing passports with a third gender option, designated with an X.

Several American states have offered residents gender-neutral options on drivers licenses, and last month, California passed a law that allows nonbinary and intersex people a nonbinary category on their birth certificates.

While much of the change worldwide has involved transgender people, the discussion has also focused attention on intersex people, those born with traits of both sexes.

"Children who are born with atypical sex characteristics are often subject to irreversible sex assignment, involuntary sterilization, involuntary genital normalizing surgery," a 2013 report from the United Nations special rapporteur on torture found, noting that they were left "with permanent, irreversible infertility and causing severe mental suffering." Human Rights Watch has condemned such procedures.

Hayley Gorenberg, general counsel at Lambda Legal, said the German ruling appeared to give parents of intersex children the option to wait until the child was old enough to determine which gender, if any, to identify with.

"It seems to be very clearly about not forcing people into a particular gender marker label, and I think that's very important," she said. "The fact is, just like any other personal characteristics, gender is on a spectrum and not everybody falls into the binary category of male or female."

The new decision comes in the case of a German citizen born in 1989 who was identified only as Vanja, by Third Option, an advocacy group that supported the plaintiff.

The German Constitution guarantees the right to personal freedom, which protects sexual identity.

"The assignment to a gender is of paramount importance for individual identity; it typically occupies a key position both in the self-image of a person and how the person is perceived by others," the court found. "It also protects the sexual identity of those persons who are neither male nor female."

Current laws that require a person to register as either male or female interfere with that right and are discriminatory, the court found.

It added that the existing law's limitation of binary gender options only to male or female was discriminatory.

The 2013 German law that allowed parents the right not to designate their child as male or female was based on a set of recommendations by the German Ethics Council that found that people who did not identify with a gender should not be forced to select one, and that "people affected should be able to decide for themselves" about their gender.

In 2014, Vanja's attempt to change her sex designation from "female" to "inter/diverse" was rejected by the registrar, who argued that such a designation was not recognized by law.

A local court also rejected Vanja's attempt to challenge the regulation. On Wednesday, the Constitutional Court overturned the lower court's ruling.

"For the first time in Germany, people who are neither male nor female are legally protected," said Moritz Schmidt, a spokesman for Third Option. "We hope that this success will be used to fight against discrimination wherever inter- and transgender people still suffer disadvantages due to their gender."

A United Nations study estimated the intersex population at 0.5 percent to 1.7 percent of the global population. In the United States, according to one estimate, transgender people made up 0.6 percent of the adult population, according to the Williams Institute at the UCLA School of Law.

"I think it's a really positive development in that it's basically the state acknowledging that bodies are diverse, and that the shoehorning of bodies into pink or blue can do a kind of violence," said Susan Stryker, an associate professor of gender and women's studies at the University of Arizona and the author of "Transgender History: The Roots of Today's Revolution," said of the Germany ruling. "But I don't necessarily see this ruling as something that's a huge victory in the battle for gender liberation. It's still very much about medicalization."

Ms. Gorenberg said of the field, "It's all moving in the same direction, but not fast enough."

MELISSA EDDY reported from Berlin, and **JESSICA BENNETT** from New York.

Queer Love in Color

BY JAMAL JORDAN | JUNE 21, 2018

Why do no gay people look like me? Jamal Jordan, a black digital editor at The Times, lamented growing up. So as an adult, he decided to give a gift to his younger self: the imagery of queer love.

AS A CHILD, I thought all gay people were white.

By the time I was 18 and living in Detroit, being gay was no longer a "problem" for me. I was out of the closet, and my family and friends were supportive, even encouraging. Yet, as I set off for college, and grew more comfortable calling myself an adult, a man — a gay black man — I was convinced that no one would ever date or love me.

Growing up, I had rarely seen queer characters of color in the gay young adult books I read, in episodes of "Queer as Folk" I watched or issues of "XY" or "Out" magazines I stealthily bought at Barnes & Noble.

JAMAL JORDAN/THE NEW YORK TIMES

Marquis, left, and Hassan at their apartment in Brooklyn.

I spent most of my teenage years believing that love between two black men wasn't even possible. To my queer white peers, an entire world of change was unfolding: Public support for same-gender marriage eventually led to its legalization nationwide, and queer people were appearing as the leads in more TV shows than I could ever watch. People even won Oscars for directing movies about gay white cowboys.

But none of these people looked like me.

How can you believe in something you've never seen?

In the decade since, the wave of change has continued. And yet: I can't think of a single high-profile example of a loving relationship between two queer people of color.

Despite taking the time to learn to love myself, building the courage to drape myself in a body-length rainbow flag and march in the Pride parade, I still didn't know what it would look like — feel like — to receive love from someone who looks like me.

Or, more important, how to give it.

So, I embarked on an adventure.

As a visual journalist, I believe pictures can connect with people in a way that other forms of media can't. To this end, I decided to give a gift to my younger self: the imagery of queer love I've never seen. Queer love in color.

HASSAN WILLIAMS AND MARQUIS FACEY
Flatbush

It was early on a Saturday morning and neither Marquis nor Hassan had eaten.

Their relationship has taken them on adventures across the world. They've supported each other through parent visits, financial hardships and hospital trips.

Standing for a few photos with empty stomachs was nothing.

After I'd gotten my pictures, and Marquis, 29, had escaped to the kitchen to make breakfast, Hassan, 27, staring into space deep in thought, broke the silence.

"I think it's important for black folks to know that we can come together and love each other in intimate, romantic, spiritual ways.

"The media will have you believe that it's literally impossible to see two queer black folks in love. But it happens."

CYREE JARELLE JOHNSON AND AZURE D OSBORNE-LEE
East New York

After growing up in an abusive household, Cyree then escaped an abusive relationship. After that, how do you love?

"The only reason, four years later, that I'm able to get married, is that I had to learn to love myself," Cyree said, emphatically, Azure holding their hand. "Only then could I make decisions as though I liked myself."

They are currently searching for a wedding venue.

Cyree, 29, and Azure, 33, identify as trans-masculine, and their commonality of experience, as Azure said, makes their relationship feel particularly like "home."

Cyree, left, and Azure, both late for appointments, outside of their home in Brooklyn.

Do you have any advice for other trans couples?

Cyree, suddenly serious, said don't get caught up in other people's conception of "love."

DOM AND NICK SPENCE
Bryant Park

Dom and Nick have attracted over 10,000 Instagram followers by chronicling their relationship and eventual marriage.

They have dated since high school, though if you asked them, they would say those years don't count. (As someone who had only a distant concept of romance until later in life, I say it totally counts.)

I wondered what it would have been like to know Dom, 28, and Nick, 26, then.

They receive messages from strangers on social media "almost every day." Many come from young people in African countries, happy to see romance between black men. Some come from parents of young queer children, mostly black, who find relief in seeing what love could look like for them.

"Everything we do on social media is genuine," Nick says. "We want people to know that everything we have is attainable for anyone."

SOFIA BERGER AND SEKIYA DORSETT
Bedford-Stuyvesant

If Sekiya still lived in the Bahamas, where she grew up, she would probably be with a man.

Why did you agree to these photos with me?

"We love being lesbians," Sekiya says. "Where I grew up, we didn't have these types of images. So it's very powerful for me."

I quickly noticed all the small ways Sekiya, 34 and Sofia, 37, take care of each other. Sofia fluffed Sekiya's Afro and wiped sweat from her brow. Sekiya grabbed Sofia and kissed her reassuringly as she rearranged the curios on her mantle (for the second time).

Sofia Berger, left, and Sekiya Dorsett. "We love being lesbians," Sekiya says. "Where I grew up, we didn't have these types of images. So it's very powerful for me."

As an interior designer, she needed the background to look perfect.

Many external forces have almost torn them apart — immigration issues, near-deportation and multiple health scares. "Sofia stuck by my side," Sekiya said. And Sekiya stayed by hers.

When you love someone, they told me, you learn how to see it through.

TREE ALEXANDER AND CARLTON ROLLE
The Bronx

I'd never met gay parents before. But I had taken a family portrait.

It's clear that Tree and Carlton have big dreams, for their family and their business — Zambo Aroma, a small shop in the North Bronx that sells soaps, candles and beard oil.

Taking photos with children is hard. At first they wouldn't look at me, then they cried. The boys ran away, then hid behind their parents before deciding to team up and attack me: One on my back, one on my leg, before everyone else joined in.

Tree, 31, and Carlton, 30, beamed through it all.

Lesson learned: Children aren't props, and this wouldn't look like a magazine spread.

On one hand, it felt just like every other family portrait. On the other, I felt like I'd captured something impossible.

PAULETTE THOMAS-MARTIN AND PAT MARTIN
Harlem

As soon as I arrived at Paulette and Pat's apartment, I was asked to open a high curtain.

Pat, sitting in a window-side chair warned, "You keep this up, and she'll have you dusting soon."

Paulette and Pat, both 66, have 13 grandchildren between them — gifts from the lives they lived before they met each other. They are old enough to be my mothers.

I never knew people of that generation who were so openly gay. So much of queerness seems to be tied up in an obsession with youth, and it's hard for me to imagine what came before that.

They live together in Harlem and speak fondly of the neighborhood that existed before familiar black faces started to disappear from the street corners, before single-family brownstones were razed for cold, metal high-rises, before the Apollo Theater was walking distance from a Whole Foods.

We walked slowly down 125th Street, Harlem's main thoroughfare, allowing the pedestrian traffic to bustle around us. A man read Bible verses on a street corner. Pat stopped to say hello. He'd been a fixture in the neighborhood since he was a child.

When I'd first moved to New York, I lived in this same neighborhood. Even then, I couldn't imagine dating someone. I could never imagine walking down 125th Street, holding his hand.

Paulette Thomas-Martin and Pat Martin live together in Harlem. They are both 66 and have 13 grandchildren between them from the lives they lived before they met.

I stopped and posed them for a picture. There, among the smell of incense and the distant sounds of a drum circle, Pat pulled Paulette close. Most people walked around us. A few bumped into me. Some stared.

Neither of them seemed to notice.

JAMAL JORDAN is an editor on The New York Times' Digital Transition team.

CHAPTER 4

Feminism

As L.G.B.T.Q.I.A. activists have advanced the interests
of individuals across the sexual spectrum, so too have
women been fighting for gender equality. Beginning in the
1960s, the Second Wave feminist movement battled for
equal pay, reproductive rights and greater representation.
As a result, they shifted cultural attitudes toward feminism.
In recent years, the #MeToo movement, inspired by the
revelations of sexual abuse in the film industry, has created a new battleground for women's rights.

The Lesbian Issue and Women's Lib

BY JUDY KLEMESRUD | **DEC. 18, 1970**

THE LESBIAN ISSUE, which has been hidden away like a demented child
ever since the women's liberation movement came into being in 1966,
was brought out of the closet yesterday.

Nine leaders of the movement held a press conference at the Washington Square Methodist Church, 133 West Fourth Street, to express
their "solidarity with the struggle of homosexuals to attain their liberation in a sexist society."

The conference was prompted by an article in the Behavior section of the December 14 issue of Time magazine, which said that Kate
Millett, author of "Sexual Politics" and one of the chief theoreticians
of the movement, had probably "discredited herself as spokeswoman
for her cause" because she disclosed at a recent meeting that she was
bisexual.

PREPARED STATEMENT IS READ

The 36-year-old Miss Millett, sitting in the center of the leaders at a table in the front of the church, read a statement that she said had been prepared last Monday night at a meeting of about 30 women representing such groups as the National Organization for Women (NOW), Radical Lesbians, Columbia Women's Liberation and Daughters of Bilitis.

The statement said, in part:

> Women's liberation and homosexual liberation are both struggling towards a common goal: A society free from defining and categorizing people by virtue of gender and/or sexual preference. 'Lesbian' is a label used as a psychic weapon to keep women locked into their male-defined 'feminine role.' The essence of that role is that a woman is defined in terms of her relationship to men. A woman is called a Lesbian when she functions autonomously. Women's autonomy is what women's liberation is all about.

Standing behind Miss Millett as she spoke were about 50 women supporters, who frequently interrupted her statement with cheers. Other leaders in the group were Gloria Steinem, the journalist; Ruth Simpson, president of the New York chapter of Daughters of Bilitis; Florynce Kennedy, a lawyer; Sally Kempton and Susan Brownmiller, journalists and members of New York Radical Feminists; and Ivy Bottini, Dolores Alexander and Ti-Grace Atkinson of NOW.

"It's not quite my position," Miss Atkinson, a tall, slender blonde in blue sunglasses said afterwards. "It's not radical enough. If men succeed in associating Lesbianism with the women's movement, then they destroy the movement."

The Lesbian issue had been festering for several months, especially since the Women's Strike for Equality last August 26.

At a rally at Bryant Park following the August 26 march down Fifth Avenue, a member of the Radical Lesbians made a plaintive plea for support from her "straight" sisters in the movement. The speaker charged that the police were harassing Lesbians, and that other women in the movement were ignoring their plight.

"We're your sisters, and we need help" the speaker cried.

The church had been decorated for the press conference with posters that read, "Kate is Great," "We Stand Together as Women, Regardless of Sexual Preference," and "Is the Statue of Liberty a Lesbian, Too?"

During the question period, Miss Alexander said she thought the movement had taken an overly long time to deal with the Lesbian issue because many women in the movement were afraid to confront it.

'SUCH AN EXPLOSIVE ISSUE'

"It's such an explosive issue," she said. "It can intimidate women. Many women would be reduced to tears if you called them Lesbians."

She added that the movement represented women who were "heterosexuals, homosexuals, tall, short, fat, skinny, black, yellow and white."

"People must speak up as Lesbians," said Barbara Love, of the Gay Liberation Front. "I am a Lesbian. We've got to come out and fight, because we're not going to get anywhere if we don't."

Miss Kennedy, the only black woman among the leaders, called for a total "girlcott" of the products of the major advertisers in Time magazine.

Although they weren't present, supporting statements were distributed from Bella Abzug, Democratic Representative-elect of the 19th Congressional District; Caroline Bird, author of "Born Female," and Aileen C. Hernandez, national president of NOW, who called the attempts to use Lesbianism as a weapon against the women's liberation movement "sexual McCarthyism."

Betty Friedan, high priestess of the women's liberation movement and conservative on the Lesbian issue, did not attend the press conference. Leaders said they had tried to contact her, but that she was "out of town."

March 22, 1998: Why Feminists Support Clinton

OPINION | BY GLORIA STEINEM | SEPT. 25, 2010

IF ALL THE sexual allegations now swirling around the White House turn out to be true, President Clinton may be a candidate for sex addiction therapy. But feminists will still have been right to resist pressure by the right wing and the news media to call for his resignation or impeachment. The pressure came from another case of the double standard.

For one thing, if the president had behaved with comparable insensitivity toward environmentalists, and at the same time remained their most crucial champion and bulwark against an anti-environmental Congress, would they be expected to desert him? I don't think so. If President Clinton were as vital to preserving freedom of speech as he is to preserving reproductive freedom, would journalists be condemned as "inconsistent" for refusing to suggest he resign? Forget it.

For another, there was and is a difference between the accusations against Mr. Clinton and those against Bob Packwood and Clarence Thomas. Commentators might stop puzzling over the president's favorable poll ratings, especially among women, if they understood the common-sense guideline to sexual behavior that came out of the women's movement 30 years ago: no means no; yes means yes.

It's the basis of sexual harassment law. It also explains why the news media's obsession with sex qua sex is offensive to some, titillating to many and beside the point to almost everybody. Like most feminists, most Americans become concerned about sexual behavior when someone's will has been violated; that is, when "no" hasn't been accepted as an answer.

Perhaps we have a responsibility to make it O.K. for politicians to tell the truth — providing they are respectful of "no means no; yes means yes" — and still be able to enter high office.

Until then, we will disqualify energy and talent the country needs.

GLORIA STEINEM is a co-founder of the Women's Media Center.

What Makes a Woman a Woman?

BY PEGGY ORENSTEIN | SEPT. 11, 2009

THERE IS A PAINTING by Richard Prince hanging in the Walker Art Center in Minneapolis, a purple canvas bisected by one line of chartreuse type that reads: "I met my first girl, her name was Sally. Was that a girl, was that a girl. That's what people kept asking." That refrain echoed in my head as I pored over the photos of 18-year-old Caster Semenya, the South African track star whose biological sex was called into question last month after she annihilated her competition, winning the 800-meter world championship in significantly less time than her own previous finishes.

Was that a girl, was that a girl. That's what people kept asking.

Semenya's saga was made for the news media. A girl who may not be a girl! That chest! Those arms! That face! She was the perfect vehicle for nearly any agenda: was this another incidence of people calling into question black female athletes' femininity (the Williams sisters, the basketball legend Sheryl Swoopes)? Was it sexist to assume women were incapable of huge leaps in athletic performance? Should all female athletes be gender-verified, as they were in Olympic competition until 1999? (The practice was dropped because no competitive edge was proved for the few women with rare disorders of sex development — it served only to humiliate them.) Should the entire practice of sex-segregating sports be abandoned?

Was that a girl, was that a girl. That's what people kept asking.

I had my own reasons to be fascinated by Semenya's story: I related to it. Not directly — I mean, no one has ever called my biological sex into question. No one, that is, except for me. After my breast-cancer diagnosis at age 35, I was told I almost certainly had a genetic mutation that predisposed me to reproductive cancers. The way I could best reduce my risk would be to surgically remove both of my breasts and my ovaries. In other words, to amputate healthy body parts. But not just any parts: the ones associated in the most primal way with repro- duction, sexuality, with my sense of myself as female. Even without that additional blow, breast cancer can feel like an assault on your fem- ininity. Reconstructing the psyche becomes as much a part of going through treatment as reconstructing the body.

In the weeks that followed my diagnosis, during that heightened, crystalline time of fear and anxiety, I was not, I admit, at my most rational. So I began to fret: without breasts or hormone-producing ovaries, what would the difference be, say, between myself and a pre-op female-to-male transsexual? Other than that my situation was involuntary? That seemed an awfully thin straw on which to base my entire sense of womanhood. What, precisely, made me a girl anyway? Who got to decide? How much did it matter?

When I was in college, in the early 1980s, the gospel was that the whole enchilada of gender was a social construct: differences between boys and girls were imposed by culture, rather than programmed by chromosomes and chemicals, and it was time to divest ourselves of them. That turned out to be less true than feminists of the era might have wished: physiology, not just sisterhood, is powerful. While fem- ininity may be relative — slipping and sliding depending on the age in which you live, your stage of life, what you're wearing (quick: do tailored clothes underscore or undercut it?) even the height of the per- son standing next to you — biology, at least to some degree, is destiny, though it should make no never mind to women's rights or progress.

Even as I went on as a journalist to explore ideas about gender, I took the fact of my own for granted: as for most people — men and women alike — it was so clear to me as to be invisible. I was unnerved, then, to discover not only that it could be so easily threatened but also how intense that threat felt. That, too, gave me pause: why should being biologically male or female still be so critical to our self-definition? Is it nature — an evolutionary imperative to signal with whom we can reproduce? Is it nurture? Either way, and regardless of our changing roles and opportunities, it is profound.

Was that a girl, was that a girl. That's what people kept asking.

And yet, identity is not simply the sum of our parts. That's what makes Semenya — whose first name is usually conferred on a boy but happens to be Greek for "beaver" — so intriguing. Science may or may not be able to establish some medical truth about her, something that will be relevant on the playing field. But I doubt that will change who she considers herself to be. According to Sheri Berenbaum, a professor of psychology and pediatrics at Penn State who studies children with disorders of sex development, even people with ambiguous biology tend to identify as male or female, though what motivates that decision remains unclear. "People's hormones matter," she said, "but something about their rearing matters too. What about it, though, no one really knows."

There is something mysterious at work, then, that makes us who we are, something internally driven. Maybe it's about our innate need to categorize the world around us. Maybe it arises from — or gives rise to — languages that don't allow for neutrality. My guess, however, is that it's deeper than that, something that transcends objectivity, defies explanation. That's what I concluded about myself, anyway. Although I have, so far, opted to hang onto my body parts (and still wonder, occasionally, if I would feel differently were, say, a kidney or an arm at issue), I know that my sex could never really be changed by any surgeon's scalpel. Why not? Perhaps because of the chemistry set I was born with, one that Semenya may or may not share. Perhaps merely because ... I say so. And maybe that will have to be enough.

PEGGY ORENSTEIN, a contributing writer, is the author of "Waiting for Daisy," a memoir.

Who Is a Feminist Now?

BY MARISA MELTZER | MAY 21, 2014

IN A RECENT INTERVIEW with Time magazine, the actress Shailene Woodley was asked if she considered herself a feminist.

"No," said Ms. Woodley, 22. "Because I love men, and I think the idea of 'raise women to power, take the men away from the power' is never going to work out because you need balance."

It was a somewhat surprising response from an actress known for portraying strong-willed women in films like "The Spectacular Now," "Divergent" and "The Fault in Our Stars," to be released soon.

"She's hardworking and talented, and the fact that she can open a movie is feminism in action," said Melissa Stack, a screenwriter who wrote "The Other Woman" (a film Ms. Woodley called "really neat" in Time for "creating a sisterhood of support for one another versus hating each other").

Ms. Woodley has a reputation for being outspoken about environmental causes and has aired her support in numerous interviews. But the online backlash to her comment about feminism came quickly.

Jennifer Weiner, 44, a novelist, took to Twitter to write, "Dear Young Actresses: Before you sound off on feminists and how you're not one, please figure out what feminism is." Zerlina Maxwell, 32, a political analyst, chimed in with, "Here's another actress rejecting a feminist label she can't define properly."

Open letters addressed to Ms. Woodley showed up on The Huffington Post and on YouTube.

"My reaction was, 'Oh, no, not again,' " said Sarah Marian Seltzer, 31, who wrote one such retort, "Dear Shailene Woodley," for the website the Hairpin. "There is this pattern of celebrities immediately saying, 'No, I'm not a feminist, I love men,' and there's not a chance for a follow-up learning experience for anyone."

Ms. Woodley's age is a likely factor in her distance, said Leonora Epstein, 28, who co-wrote the generational guide "X vs. Y: A Culture War, a Love Story." Ms. Epstein said that, "She's technically a millennial, but a young one, and it makes me wonder if they grew up with less oppression, and therefore never felt they needed a tool like feminism to fight or empower."

The writer Jessica Grose took a more laissez-faire view, writing on Elle.com that journalists should stop asking actresses whether they're feminists.

"It feels like a game of gotcha," Ms. Grose, 32, said in an interview. "She's not the enemy here."

Whether a woman in the public eye calls herself a feminist is an exercise in semiotics, she said, and the hesitation among celebrities to fully embrace the cause is a fear that: " 'If I don't say the exact right thing or express it in the right way, I'll be rejected.' It makes the movement seem judgmental or unwelcoming."

Andi Zeisler, 41, a founder of the feminist pop culture magazine Bitch, said, "Just the fact that these questions are being asked shows that feminism is a lot more accepted." The problem, she said, is that some celebrities do not know what the core values and goals of feminism are.

"I don't care if people don't identify as feminist," Ms. Zeisler said. She does have a problem with misinformation and the perpetuation of the idea that feminism is "this zero-sum game that if it elevates women, then it denigrates men. That's just wrong and has never been what feminism is about. That's the Fox News version of feminism."

Over the last year, feminism has achieved a certain ubiquity in pop culture. Last October, Glamour magazine published an article with the title "The New Do: Calling Yourself a Feminist." Sheryl Sandberg, 44, the chief operating officer of Facebook and the author of "Lean In," told HuffPost Live in April: "I embrace the word 'feminism.' I didn't do it earlier in my career and I talk about why in the book, but I embrace it now because what feminism is, is a belief that the world should be equal, that men and women should have equal opportunity."

As was widely discussed in social media, Beyoncé, 32, also had a form of feminist coming-out last winter. She had previously flirted with the term, telling British Vogue last spring, "I guess I am a modern-day feminist." But she also added, "Why do you have to choose what type of woman you are? Why do you have to label yourself anything? I'm just a woman, and I love being a woman."

By the December release of her album "Beyoncé," one song on it, "Flawless," sampled the TED talk of the author Chimamanda Ngozi Adichie titled "We Should All Be Feminists," and includes a quote from it: "Feminist: the person who believes in the social, political and economic equality of the sexes." And in January, the singer wrote a post entitled "Gender Equality Is a Myth!" for The Shriver Report.

Ms. Zeisler pointed to Beyoncé as a celebrity who "publicly grappled with feminism and found her own path to it — that's the right way to do it, rather than denigrating it, which is what happens with these sound bites."

Beyond the confines of Hollywood, American women appear to be warming to the term; according to a study by Ms. Magazine, the number of women calling themselves feminists increased from 50 percent in 2006 to 68 percent in 2012.

But ambivalence like Ms. Woodley's is as much a part of the discussion. Monica Lewinsky, 40, wrote in Vanity Fair's June issue, "Given my experience of being passed around like gender-politics cocktail food, I don't identify myself as a Feminist, capital F."

And she is joined by a host of other celebrities who question the usage, including Lady Gaga, 28, who was quoted telling a Norwegian camera crew, "I'm not a feminist! I love men! I hail men." Kelly Clarkson, 32, told Time last October, "I think when people hear feminist, it's like, 'Get out of my way, I don't need anyone'." Carrie Underwood, Katy Perry, Carla Bruni, Sandra Day O'Connor and Taylor Swift have similarly distanced themselves from the designation during their careers.

When Marissa Mayer, 38, the chief executive of Yahoo, appeared in the PBS/AOL documentary "Makers," she spoke of her own issues with the term.

"I don't think that I would consider myself a feminist," she said. "I think that, I certainly believe in equal rights. I believe that women are just as capable, if not more so, in a lot of different dimensions. But I don't, I think, have sort of the militant drive and sort of the chip on the shoulder that sometimes comes with that."

In response, some celebrities have gone out of their way in interviews to express bafflement with women who won't say they are feminists. Lena Dunham, 28, told Metro UK in early 2013 that her "greatest pet peeve" was women spurning the term. Last summer in The Guardian, Ellen Page, 27, said: "I don't know why people are so reluctant to say they're feminists. Maybe some women just don't care. But how could it be any more obvious that we still live in a patriarchal world when feminism is a bad word?"

The actress Amy Poehler, 42, told Elle earlier this year: "Some big actors and musicians feel like they have to speak to their audience and that word is confusing to their audience. But I don't get it. That's like someone being like, 'I don't really believe in cars, but I drive one every day and I love that it gets me places and makes life so much easier and faster and I don't know what I would do without it.' "

The problem is really whether a famous person is simply checking the feminist box, said Roxane Gay, the author of an essay collection "Bad Feminist," which comes out this summer.

"Forty years ago it was a good question, but in 2014 it's a ridiculous question and a lazy question," said Ms. Gay, 39. "As culture critics, we have to start advancing the conversation and asking questions that are more grounded in feminism, like 'How does feminism shape your life?' "

In fact, in "Who Needs Feminism," a photography project that originated at Duke University in 2012, students posed with notecards with their answers to the question, "Who needs feminism?" The phrasing was paramount, said Rachel F. Seidman, an adjunct assistant professor of history and women's and gender studies at the University of North Carolina who was teaching a course at Duke.

"The students decided to do a p.r. campaign for feminism as their final project," Dr. Seidman said. "The idea was everybody should be able to complete this sentence, 'I need feminism because....' By phrasing it that way, rather than claiming it as an identity, young people were able to say this is a tool kit I can use without making it be 'this is who I am and this is only who I am.' That was key in why this became so popular so fast."

But there is value in public figures taking up the movement, said Martha Plimpton, 43, an actress who, like Ms. Woodley, became famous during her teenage years.

"I take a lot of pride in calling myself a feminist and always have," she wrote in an email. "We're going to have to insist on correcting bigotry as it happens, in real time. And fear of women's equality, or the diminishment of it, is a kind of bigotry. I think it's important to remove the stigma associated with women's equality, and as such, yes, normalizing the word 'feminist' and making sure people know what it means is incredibly important, whether we're talking to celebrities or anyone."

When a Feminist Pledges a Sorority

BY JESSICA BENNETT | APRIL 9, 2016

IT WAS A THURSDAY evening on the Columbia University campus, and a group from the Kappa Alpha Theta sorority was wedged onto couches eating takeout, some seated cross-legged on the floor. Two discussed an introductory Chinese language class. One thanked a sister for passing along her résumé for an internship. And then there were a few talking about spring break.

They had gone to Cabo, that cliché of a college pilgrimage in which a once-sleepy Mexican village becomes a hormone-fueled frat row, and you never, ever let your drink out of your sight (and if you do, you dump it). Except the women weren't recounting drunken hookups or how many shots they'd taken on the beach. They were discussing "toxic masculinity," the "privilege" that allowed them to be there and the "risk team" they put in place to look out for one another if anybody got too drunk or separated from their group.

When, at a beachside bar, a drunken bachelor tried to playfully bite — yes, bite — one of the women's arms ("Who does that?" she asked), they staged an intervention. "What makes you think she wants to be touched?" her friend said, girl posse in tow, lecturing him on respectful personal space.

Later, when they stumbled upon a twerking contest on the beach (women twerking, the crowd judging), one in the group couldn't help herself. "Don't you find it problematic that there are no men up there?" she said to any stranger who would listen. "I think we felt empowered to speak up because we knew we had each other's backs," she recalled, seated on a sorority house sofa.

She later posted photos from the trip to Facebook: girlfriends with bronzed shoulders, guacamole and a casual shot of her beach read: "The Grounding of Modern Feminism," by the Harvard historian Nancy F. Cott.

Kappa Alpha Theta members at Columbia. From left, Amulya Kandikonda, Katherine Milne, Natalie Bacon, Georgie Jones and Jing Qu.

There was a time, not so long ago, when no self-respecting feminist would be caught dead in a sorority. "In my day? No way in hell!" said Sally Roesch Wagner, a women's studies scholar at Syracuse University, who graduated in 1969. "Sororities represented to me as a feminist what beauty pageants did: women who were caught in the 'get pretty, party, get a guy, get married' syndrome that we were trying to break out of."

That was certainly my stance back in 2002, as a sophomore at the University of Southern California. I transferred colleges, in large part because I so detested that school's suffocating Greek life — giving up a scholarship, taking out a loan and moving to a city I'd never visited to try to find friends (and a social life) I didn't have to "pay" for. Sororities, at least the traditional ones, were precisely the kind of classist, exclusionary groups that feminists fought against. Right?

It is puzzling, then, to discover that even amid the debate about campus sexual assault, and the role that Greek life plays in it, sorority enrollment is at a record high.

At the 26 historically white sororities that make up the century-old National Panhellenic Conference — and to be clear, this group does not include academic or multicultural sororities, like the popular African-American or Latino groups, which have their own governing bodies — enrollment has increased more than 50 percent over the last decade, outpacing the growth in college enrollment. And not just on the campuses you'd expect. At the Ivies — those institutions that long considered themselves just a hair too progressive for the pomp and ritual of sorority life; where women rushed to "The Vagina Monologues," not the local frat mixer.

Harvard doesn't even recognize Greek life on campus, yet this is the third year in a row that sorority enrollment has peaked, with 280 women seeking entrance to one of the college's four chapters this year.

DINA LITOVSKY FOR THE NEW YORK TIMES

Jing Qu, a Columbia University junior and Kappa Alpha Thea member. Nationally, sorority membership has never been higher, thanks in part to an embrace of feminism.

Of those who rushed, 193 were offered bids, "a significant increase from the 150 women that constituted the average rush class size before 2011," The Harvard Crimson wrote.

The numbers are similar at Brown, a place where Greek life was long considered so insignificant that a 2002 graduate, when asked about the trend, said, "Brown has sororities?" (This year, 293 Brown women rushed, about a 42 percent increase over last year.)

And at Yale, students voted to bring a fourth sorority to campus this year to contend with growing demand. "I believe it, women flocking to sororities, but it's depressing," said Kristin Houser, a Seattle lawyer and a 1971 Yale graduate. "I think the world feels so overwhelming that people want to return to traditions that seem comforting and provide structure and social support. But there was a reason that we rebelled against all of that."

And then there are the New York schools: all-women's Barnard, which banned sororities in 1916, calling them "elitist," and Columbia, where a recent student newspaper article, "35 Ways You Know You're a Columbia Student," listed No. 26: "OMG YOU WOULD NEVER GO TO A FRAT PARTY. You are so above Greek life."

Except that actually you probably would go to a frat party (see No. 27: "Sorry, how did you end up at Beta house?") because sorority enrollment is unprecedented at Columbia, too — more than tripling over the last decade, "a growth unmatched by fraternities or multi-cultural groups," according to The Columbia Spectator. At Barnard — which allows students to pledge at neighboring Columbia — 20 percent of the student body is Greek, according to the Columbia Panhellenic Council, which monitors sorority life on campus.

It has left many people baffled. "Honestly, when she first brought it up, my interior reaction was, 'Over my dead body!' That's how strongly I felt that Greek life was an abomination," said Susan Ruderman, a 1984 graduate of Harvard College, whose 18-year-old daughter — in the midst of the college application process — informed her that she was considering rushing. Ms. Ruderman, who works in philanthropy in Newton,

Mass., said her first thought was: "Where did I go wrong?" — though she has slowly come around. "Funny how much principles 'evolve' when it comes to the happiness of one's daughter," she said.

When Amulya Kandikonda, a Barnard sophomore, told her friends back home in Illinois that she was pledging, "They were like, 'You're not white, you're not tall and blond,' " she said. Which was not dissimilar from the experience of her sorority sister, Jennifer Egbebike, whose parents are Nigerian, but who grew up in Miami. "I was very hesitant to join, because I'm not a 'typical' sorority girl," she said.

"Every year, we graduate these incredibly strong, talented, creative, activist women — proud feminists — and then they come back home to visit, and they've pledged," said the historian Barbara Berg, a women's history teacher at an all-girls private school in Manhattan and the author of "Sexism in America: Alive, Well, and Ruining Our Future." "I was surprised, but over and over again I hear the same thing: It's not as exclusionary as it used to be, it's supportive, and it's going to lead to other possibilities after graduation."

"What I would love to think is that it's not your mother's sorority anymore. That it has evolved."

On some campuses, anyway, that may be true. Words like "safe space," "hegemonic masculinity" and "intersectionality" roll off these women's tongues. Gone are the campy sorority jobs of yore — replaced by titles like "C.E.O.," "C.O.O." and "Chief Marketing Officer" to look better on a résumé. They read each other's cover letters and tell each other to "send me your résumé, I'll pass it along,' " said Oladunni Ogundipe, a Columbia senior. They are also in the midst of a robust debate about transgender inclusion.

"There are a lot of us who say openly that we are feminist, but even when we don't, I think it's implied in our interactions," said Julia Wu, a Brown junior who is originally from Brazil. She recently hosted a "Lean In" workshop at her sorority, which she opened by telling the group, "There are more men named John than there are women who run companies in this country."

At Theta at Columbia, "sisterhood events" — monthly camaraderie-building gatherings that are typical of sororities — take the form of presidential debate watching parties and a recent alumni networking brunch. There is no "pomping" — a ritual that involves weaving tissue paper to create elaborate floats and displays. But there are mandatory workshops on sexual consent and bystander intervention.

"I grew up in the South, so going to college I never expected to be a part of a sorority because I did think it was antifeminist," said Blair Wilson, a Columbia sophomore. "But when I came to school, all the women I looked up to — those involved in student government, in sexual violence response, in different political groups — were involved."

Last year, as Columbia erupted in debate over Emma Sulkowicz — the student who carried a mattress around campus to protest the university's handling of their sexual assault complaint — members of the chapter signed their names to a donated mattress and carried it to a rally in support.

DINA LITOVSKY FOR THE NEW YORK TIMES

Blair Wilson reads Roxane Gay's "Bad Feminist," at Barnard College.

"We definitely still have to defend ourselves," said a Barnard sophomore, Ilina Odouard, a neuroscience and behavior major. "But I almost feel more into feminism after having joined Theta than going to Barnard."

Sororities did in fact begin as feminist organizations — a way for women, in the early days of coeducation, to band together inside hostile institutions. As the historian Diana Turk has chronicled in her book, "Bound by a Mighty Vow: Sisterhood and Women's Fraternities, 1870-1920," the first known Greek letter sorority — or "women's fraternity," as it was known — was formed in 1870. The early organizations were not overtly political, but their members often were: active in the suffrage movement, determined, as Ms. Turk put it, to prove themselves intellectual equals to men.

"This was a time when female students often had to sit in the back of the classroom, when they were often ignored by the male faculty, or addressed as 'Mr.,' even in coed institutions," Ms. Turk said. "So I know that that can sound strange to some people, that early sororities acted in feminist manners before feminist was even a word, but these were women who were really trying to expand the boundaries of what was considered O.K. for women to do."

It was later, in the early 1900s, that the social aspect (parties, mixers) and outwardly exclusionary policies of these groups began to make it on the books, said Ms. Turk — a result of education access expanding beyond the white upper class (and, thus, a need to keep those other women out). These policies would give rise to the first African-American and Jewish sororities — founded at Howard University and Barnard — which remain vibrant today.

But among the traditionally white groups, residuals of that history, and modern twists to it, remain: As recently as three years ago, two black women were denied sorority entry at the University of Alabama; at my alma mater, a recruitment email was recently leaked, containing a PowerPoint of 25 different shades of turquoise and the nine that members were allowed to wear (yes to "bezique," no to "aqueduct"). Tales of binge drinking, bullying, hazing ... the list goes on.

"On the first day of my recruitment weekend, I was greeted by about 40 sisters in matching outfits and heels," said Anushua Bhattacharya, a Columbia senior who wrote an article about deactivating from Sigma Delta Tau. "I returned to my room that night feeling as if I had just finished the first round of a beauty pageant."

Even at progressive campuses, tradition remains: fines for missing meetings; elaborate rituals; bans on serving alcohol at parties — putting fraternities in control of social life. And, of course, the barrier to entry: the class issues, the cost; being chosen, or cut, based on no formal criteria.

"It's kind of like the white wedding," said Caitlin Flanagan, an author who spent a year investigating fraternity life for The Atlantic. "You see these really empowered women, feminists, and you're like: 'Wait, your dad is walking you down the aisle? What?! And the guy you've been living with has to go and ask him permission?' "

The setup of Panhellenic sororities is complicated, but it's not unlike Ms. Flanagan's analogy — involving multiple governing bodies, bylaws and constitutions that sometimes haven't been updated in a century. So while Columbia women can, for instance, individually reach out in support of Ms. Bhattacharya, who wrote about deactivating, they will also tell her they've been advised not to share the article on Facebook. The women of Brown may decide, as part of a student vote, to open up its system to transgender women, but the national chapters of the sororities could institute their own policies at any point. These groups can work to diversify their membership — and in many cases, they have — but most are still governed by a majority of white women more than twice their age.

"It's difficult for sororities to move forward when some influential adults' warped values are holding them back," said Alexandra Robbins, a Yale alumni and the author of "Pledged: The Secret Life of Sororities." "They can be as progressive as they want, but at the end of the day, nationals can still say, 'You have to wear makeup or look a certain way.' "

For generations past, perhaps the only way to reconcile that gap would have been to reject the system. To opt out. "To us, it just seemed like one more way of the white male establishment consolidating its power, and we were having none of it," said Ms. Houser, the Yale graduate.

Yet nearly every American president has been involved in Greek life. Fraternity alumni make up a large chunk of Fortune 500 C.E.O.s. Tales of frat-house-startups-turned-Silicon-Valley-successes (think Snapchat, Facebook, Instagram), as well as secret Wall Street handshakes, are simply par for the course.

And so: If you're an ambitious Ivy League woman, if you buy into the belief that the best way to fight the system is to grasp power within it — or, as one woman put it, "tear down the patriarchy from the inside" — then maybe, as Ms. Robbins suggested, it's no surprise "you'd want to counter what's clearly a thriving, successful old-boys network."

Ms. Berg said, "Perhaps part of this allure is that women want that network, too."

Last year, when it was revealed that the National Panhellenic Conference — along with its fraternity equivalent, the North-American Interfraternity Conference — had spent thousands lobbying for a campus sexual assault bill, several sororities broke rank to come out in protest, pressuring the N.P.C. to withdraw its support. (The bill, called the Safe Campus Act, would have blocked colleges from investigating sexual assault claims unless a victim also reported the crime to law enforcement.)

At Dartmouth, a number of sororities have "gone local," or disaffiliated from their national chapters, giving up funding in order to create their own rules. (At one, Sigma Delta, women hold parties with alcohol, with female bartenders, female door monitors and women designated to remain sober and monitor the scene.)

Other groups have said they've removed portions of their rituals — say, a reading from the New Testament — in an effort to be more inclusive. When, at one sorority, an invite to a "crush event" indicated that members needed to bring a male date, members pushed back — and the policy was changed to allow a date of any gender (or no gender, or date, at all).

When the women of Columbia's Theta chapter decided to decorate that mattress, standing front and center at a rally on campus, they made the conscious choice to use the sorority's motto — "Leading Women" — rather than their Greek letters, so as not to cause a stir within their national office.

"One could argue, that as feminists, maybe we should push back, maybe we should be trying to tear down these systems of supposed oppression," said Annika Reno, a human rights and political science major at Barnard, who gathered recently with a group of sorority women to discuss feminism and Greek life. Hosanna Fuller, a senior majoring in computer science, added: "What if the goal was changing how Greek life operates as a whole? Like what are our actual goals? How can we track success?"

"I was saying all through recruitment to anyone who would listen, 'I'm going to get in this system and I'm going to turn it on its head,' " said Jamie Fass, a Barnard first year and new pledge. "I think the world is working in a way where if we want to be competitive, it's better to be competitive within the system."

"It is an imperfect system for sure," echoed Jing Qu, a political science and women's studies major at Columbia. "But I think our generation is working to change it from the inside."

What to Ask a Celebrity Instead of 'Are You a Feminist?'

OPINION | BY JESSA CRISPIN | FEB. 25, 2017

NOW THAT FEMINISM is fashionable, it is common to ask female celebrities on the red carpet or elsewhere whether they would describe themselves as feminist. Is Jennifer Lawrence a feminist? Yes! Is Meryl Streep a feminist? She prefers the word "humanist," but I think that still counts, so yes! Is Lana del Rey a feminist? No! Is Beyoncé a feminist? Yes!

After the world of celebrity journalism concludes this very important investigative work, the feminism-lite online world maintains clickbaity lists of 33 Celebrities Who Stood Up for Feminism and 17 Celebrities Who Are Wrong About Feminism and 22 Celebrities Who Have Cellulite … oh, I guess that last one isn't relevant, although it contains a lot of the same names.

It used to be that celebrities ran from the word "feminist." It could be box office poison, like a milder version of what could happen if a leading man came out as gay. Suddenly audiences who had no trouble imagining the star as a green-skinned superhero who can travel through the core of the earth were like: "But now he's making out with a chick? Is this chemistry even believable?"

Same with feminism. The old feminist archetype — a rejection of all hair products, the swollen bellies and bosoms of the Venus de Willendorf, and oh my god I don't think they even wear high heels — was at odds with the gazelle-like stature we prefer for female celebrities.

That has changed. There has been an aggressive marketing campaign within the feminist community to make it less scary, more sexy. As a result, more women are likely to call themselves feminist, but the word has also lost most of its meaning.

Beyoncé performs in front of a "Feminist" sign. But she is a brazen capitalist who gives private concerts for the executives of corporations like Uber, a company that has a long history of labor and sexual harassment violations. She has been accused of borrowing the work of some female artists, including the choreographer Anne Teresa De Keersmaeker, or being slow to attribute their work.

What does it mean that she calls herself a feminist? Does it just mean she believes in her ability to make money? Why do we look to famous women to tell us how to feel about feminism?

Celebrity feminism is part of a self-empowerment fantasy that takes our history of oppression and our desire for liberation and uses it to sell us products. You will be set free with this pop star's album, this waterproof eyeliner, this $200 sweatshirt printed with a feminist slogan. Some celebrities' claims of feminism are backed up with work that tries to change the boys club culture of the entertainment world. Nicole Kidman's production company hires women writers and producers and actively works to expand the actresses' roles beyond the girlfriend, the wife and the victim. But for the most part it's just something to say in an interview. Yes, I'm a feminist, just don't ask me to define that.

So next time an actress is trying to promote a film, a pop star is trying to promote a record, a "real housewife" is trying to cross-promote some bizarre venture, rather than asking them whether or not they're a feminist, mix it up a little! It's Oscar Sunday, the stars are all around, #askhermore.

Here are eight questions to ask your favorite female celebrity — or male celebrity, they are easily adaptable — to get beyond the label and get at the content of their beliefs.

1. Oh, don't worry, I'm not going to ask you to justify why you're making a movie with a man who was recently arrested for domestic abuse! None of my business. But when was the last time you chose to work with a female director, producer, director of photography, writer or key grip?

2. As your body is setting the standards for beauty among preteen girls who also want to be pretty and loved, how hungry are you right now?

3. I love your new line of girl power T-shirts! So chic. Do you know how much the Bangladeshi women and children who sewed them were paid for their labor?

4. If you say you are a feminist, are you more of a bell hooks feminist? A Shulamith Firestone feminist? No, no, Shulamith Firestone, the writer, not a juice cleanse. O.K., well, are you an Emma Goldman feminist?

5. Let's do a multiple choice! I want to know if your feminism is intersectional. Here are five possible definitions for the word "intersectional" — give it your best shot.

6. Do you know how much your male co-stars are making? Do you know how much the cleaning women on set are making?

7. What is the carbon footprint on your private jet?

8. Oh, so you're thinking of moving to Canada now that Donald Trump is president? Do you think your life, insulated from his policies by your fame and money, has been affected by his administration?

Yes, let's ask her more. And when someone offers herself as an aspirational feminist figure, let's just see if she truly is someone to aspire to be.

JESSA CRISPIN is the author of "Why I Am Not a Feminist: A Feminist Manifesto."

America Made Me a Feminist

OPINION | BY PAULINA PORIZKOVA | JUNE 10, 2017

I USED TO THINK the word "feminist" reeked of insecurity. A woman who needed to state that she was equal to a man might as well be shouting that she was smart or brave. If you were, you wouldn't need to say it. I thought this because back then, I was a Swedish woman.

I was 9 when I first stepped into a Swedish school. Freshly arrived from Czechoslovakia, I was bullied by a boy for being an immigrant. My one friend, a tiny little girl, punched him in the face. I was impressed. In my former country, a bullied girl would tattle or cry. I looked around to see what my new classmates thought of my friend's feat, but no one seemed to have noticed. It didn't take long to understand that in Sweden, my power was suddenly equal to a boy's.

In Czechoslovakia, women came home from a long day of work to cook, clean and serve their husbands. In return, those women were cajoled, ignored and occasionally abused, much like domestic animals. But they were mentally unstable domestic animals, like milk cows that could go berserk if you didn't know exactly how to handle them.

In Sweden, the housekeeping tasks were equally divided. Soon my own father was cleaning and cooking as well. Why? He had divorced my mother and married a Swedish woman.

As high school approached, the boys wanted to kiss us and touch us, and the girls became a group of benevolent queens dispensing favors. The more the boys wanted us, the more powerful we became. When a girl chose to bestow her favors, the lucky boy was envied and celebrated. Slut shaming? What's a slut?

Condoms were provided by the school nurse without question. Sex education taught us the dangers of venereal diseases and unwanted pregnancy, but it also focused on fun stuff like masturbation. For a girl to own her sexuality meant she owned her body, she owned herself. Women could do anything men did, but they could also — when they chose to — bear children. And that made us more powerful than men. The word "feminist" felt antiquated; there was no longer a use for it.

When I moved to Paris at 15 to work as a model, the first thing that struck me was how differently the men behaved. They opened doors for me, they wanted to pay for my dinner. They seemed to think I was too delicate, or too stupid, to take care of myself.

Instead of feeling celebrated, I felt patronized. I claimed my power the way I had learned in Sweden: by being sexually assertive. But Frenchmen don't work this way. In discos, I'd set my eye on an attractive stranger, and then dance my way over to let him know he was a chosen one. More often than not, he fled. And when he didn't run, he asked how much I charged.

In France, women did have power, but a secret one, like a hidden stiletto knife. It was all about manipulation: the sexy vixen luring the man to do her bidding. It wasn't until I reached the United States, at 18, and fell in love with an American man that I truly had to rearrange my cultural notions.

It turned out most of America didn't think of sex as a healthy habit or a bargaining tool. Instead, it was something secret. If I mentioned masturbation, ears went red. Orgasms? Men made smutty remarks, while women went silent. There was a fine line between the private and the shameful. A former gynecologist spoke of the weather when doing a pelvic exam, as if I were a Victorian maiden who'd rather not know where all my bits were.

In America, a woman's body seemed to belong to everybody but herself. Her sexuality belonged to her husband, her opinion of herself belonged to her social circles, and her uterus belonged to the government. She was supposed to be a mother and a lover and a career woman (at a fraction of the pay) while remaining perpetually youthful and slim. In America, important men were desirable. Important women had to be desirable. That got to me.

In the Czech Republic, the nicknames for women, whether sweet or bitter, fall into the animal category: little bug, kitten, old cow, swine.

In Sweden, women are rulers of the universe. In France, women are dangerous objects to treasure and fear. For better or worse, in those countries, a woman knows her place.

But the American woman is told she can do anything and then is knocked down the moment she proves it. In adapting myself to my new country, my Swedish woman power began to wilt. I joined the women around me who were struggling to do it all and failing miserably. I now have no choice but to pull the word "feminist" out of the dusty drawer and polish it up.

My name is Paulina Porizkova, and I am a feminist.

PAULINA PORIZKOVA, a former supermodel, is the author of the novel "A Model Summer."

The Patriarchs Are Falling. The Patriarchy Is Stronger Than Ever.

OPINION | BY SUSAN FALUDI | DEC. 28, 2017

IT WOULD BE EASY to end 2017 with the impression that, whatever its afflictions, it was at least a game-changing year for feminism.

"The Female Revolution Is Here" and could "Smash Patriarchy at Its Core," social and mainstream media headlines declared. "We are blowing the whistle on the prime directive of the master/slave relationship between women and men." "This is the end of patriarchy" — this from Forbes! — "the male domination of humanity." Twitter, the newsstand and the street concur: This year witnessed a transformational moment in American sexual politics.

Surely the results of the #MeToo phenomenon are worthy. It's a seriously good thing Harvey Weinstein is gone and that the potential Harvey Weinsteins will think twice or thrice or a thousand times before harassing women whose fortunes they control. But "the end of patriarchy"? Look around.

This month, President Trump signed into law a tax bill that throws a bomb at women. The Tax Cuts and Jobs Act systematically guts benefits that support women who need support the most: It means an end to personal and dependent exemptions (a disaster for minimum-wage workers, nearly two-thirds of whom are women). An expiration date for child-care tax credits and a denial of such credits for immigrant children without Social Security cards. An end to the Affordable Care Act's individual mandate. And, barely avoided, thanks to Democrats' objections: an enshrinement of "fetal personhood" in the form of college savings accounts for unborn children, a sly grenade lobbed at legal abortion.

Not to mention that Republican congressmen plan to pay down the enormous federal deficit the bill will incur by slashing entitlements that, again, are critical to women: Medicaid (covering nearly half the births in the nation and 75 percent of family planning), Medicare (more than half of beneficiaries 65 and older — and two-thirds of those 85 and older — are women) and so on.

And that's on top of all the other Trump administration insults: reviving the global gag rule on abortion, suspending tracking of the gender wage gap, deep-sixing the Fair Pay and Safe Workplaces executive order and much more.

Which leads me to wonder, if we get rid of a handful of Harveys while losing essential rights and protections for millions of women, are we really winning this thing? How is this female calamity happening in the midst of the Female Revolution? An answer may lie in a schism that has haunted women's protest for 150 years.

American women's activism has historically taken two forms. One is an expression of direct anger at the ways individual men use and abuse us. It's righteous outrage against the unambiguous enemy with a visible face, the male predator who feeds on our vulnerability and relishes our humiliation. Mr. Weinstein's face is the devil's face du jour, and the #MeToo campaign fits squarely in this camp. The other form is less spectacular but as essential: It's fighting the ways the world is structurally engineered against women. Tied to that fight is the difficult and ambiguous labor of building an equitable system within which women have the wherewithal and power to lead full lives.

The clarion cry against individual male predation and the push for broader gender equality may seem part and parcel, especially now. When Donald Trump is the titular head of the machine, it's tempting to imagine that the machine itself has orange hair — and that to defeat Harvey Weinstein is to win. But the patriarchy is bigger than the patriarch.

The two forms of women's protest intersect, of course. Just ask generations of female workers at Ford Motor Company, who know that workplace sexual harassment undergirds a system of oppression. But fighting the patriarch and fighting the patriarchy are also distinct — and the former tends to be more popular than the latter. It's easier to mobilize against a demon, as every military propagandist — and populist demagogue — knows. It's harder, and less electrifying, to forge the terms of peace. Declaring war is thrilling. Nation building isn't.

How this plays out in feminism has been evident since the 19th century, when American women started the "social purity" movement against prostitution and "white slavery" of girls. The most popular women's mobilization of the 19th century wasn't for suffrage — it was for Prohibition, a moral crusade against demon men drinking demon rum, blowing their paychecks at the saloon and coming home to beat and rape their wives. The Women's Christian Temperance Union quickly became the nation's largest women's organization.

Did that war against men behaving badly feed into the larger battle for women's equality? In many ways, yes: Susan B. Anthony herself began as a temperance organizer. But a good number of women who railed against alcohol's evils shrank from women's suffrage. Fighting against male drunkenness fell within the time-honored female purview of defending the family and the body; extending women's rights into a new political realm felt more radical and less immediate. Frances Willard, the temperance union's formidable second president, eventually brought the organization around to supporting the female franchise by redefining the women's vote as a "home protection" issue: "citizen mothers," as the morally superior sex, would purge social degeneracy from the domestic and public circle. But Willard's attempt to further conjoin morality efforts with the second form of activism — her "Do Everything" campaign for a shorter workweek, a living wage, health care and prison reform, among other things — was snuffed out upon her death, as the union's leadership abandoned its support for broader social reform.

The challenge today is the one faced by Anthony and Willard: how to bring the outrage over male malfeasance to bear on the more far-reaching campaign for women's equality. Too often, the world's attention seems to have room for only the first. A few weeks ago on a chilly morning in Pittsburgh, two women named Chelsey Engel and

Lindsey Disler chained themselves to the entrance of the building that houses Senator Pat Toomey's local office to protest the tax bill. "The situation is so catastrophic and so dire," Ms. Disler said, her scarf-swathed torso shackled to the doors. "Something has to be done." She delivered her words to two dozen onlookers and a few police officers, who, by 8:30 a.m., had sent the two women packing. Their protest barely registered outside a few area news outlets, on a day when the media was aflutter with reports of the latest celebrity accused of harassment, Peter Martins, director of New York City Ballet.

The two forms of female protest can even be positioned against each other. In the 1980s, the "War on Pornography" campaign set off the damaging "sex wars" within the women's movement itself, at the very moment when a backlash against women's equality was amassing its forces and Ronald Reagan's administration was formulating policies that would disproportionately hurt half the country. The "sex-positive" feminists who worried about restrictions on free speech and questioned the condemnation of all pornographic material found themselves labeled, by anti-pornography feminists, as shills and pimps for the industry. Today we're already seeing the long knives come out for sister travelers who have called for some due process and proportionality in confronting male harassers.

A similar quarrel surfaced in Hillary Clinton's defeat last year. Some feminist-minded women deemed her an unacceptable choice to pursue the art of dealing and compromising necessary to running the state — and running it to the greater benefit of women — because she'd already compromised herself by staying with, and defending, Bill Clinton.

The forces behind this divide are so intractable in part because they are so psychological. To fight the devil is to be on the side of the angels, to assume the mantle of virtue and purity. The political arena, by contrast, is no place for angels, and its victories are slow and often incomplete. Without gainsaying the courage of "silence breakers," one can note the flip side: that their words, especially now, can generate instant, and dramatic, response — and more immediate gratification than one gets from protesting economic and legal structures.

Since Mr. Trump's election, women have been trying hard to fight on both fronts. The #MeToo campaign exists alongside the Women's March on Washington, black female voters sending an Alabama Democrat to the Senate, and a stunning number of female candidates seeking office in coming elections. If women can break the hex that has kept them from harnessing the pure politics of personal outrage to the impure politics of society building, then maybe our Chelsey Engels and Lindsey Dislers can draw as much attention to their protest as the next actress will outing the next loathsome boss.

That paradigm shift will be critical to winning the coming battles for women's rights: health insurance, pay equity, family planning, sexual assault, and more. The peril is that activist women won't transcend the divide. In which case, #MeToo will continue to topple patriarchs, while the patriarchy continues to win the day.

SUSAN FALUDI is the author, most recently, of "In the Darkroom."

CHAPTER 5

Sexual Consent and Behavior

As cultural attitudes toward gender and sexuality have shifted, so too has sex itself. From debates over monogamy to the murky waters of sexual consent, the intersection between sex and sexuality continues to be dynamic and a source of debate. The articles in this chapter show the evolution of reporting on sexual behaviors and patterns and how individuals, tech companies and universities have contributed to cultural behaviors and social mores.

Group Sex: Is It 'Life Art' or a Sign That Something Is Wrong?

BY ENID NEMY | MAY 10, 1971

CHANGING SEXUAL PATTERNS are posing new problems for marriage counselors. The most recent development is group sex.

"It's either a growing phenomenon or people are talking about it more openly. It's all over the country," said Dr. Wardell Pomeroy, past president of the American Association of Marriage and Family Counselors.

Dr. Pomeroy, a co-author of the Kinsey Reports, said an increasing number of participants in group sex were consulting him professionally. One anthropologist has estimated that by late 1970, between 1 and 2 million people were involved.

The number seeking help is still relatively small, and the issue of group sex (sexual activities involving three or more people; it often means partner exchange or the involvement of many couples in one place at one time) is often only one of a number of conflicts in a marriage. It has, however, become of sufficient importance to warrant the attention of marriage counseling groups.

THE GROWTH IN the number of couples mentioning group sex when they visit professional counselors was indicated by Mrs. Carolyn Symonds, a graduate student in sociology at the University of California in Riverside.

Mrs. Symonds, who chose group sex as the subject for her master's thesis, was asked to write an article on it for the quarterly magazine published by the California State Marriage Counseling Association and is currently speaking to workshops of the association in various cities.

"These counselors are being confronted with clients interested or involved," she said. "What's happening now is that group sex is becoming more open. It's coming above ground."

The American Psychopathological Association in New York was told earlier this spring that "it would seem that participants in co-marital sex have taken the spousal and familial 'togetherness' emphasized in the late 1950's a step further than anticipated or intended."

Lynn G. and James R. Smith, the authors of the report, teach a course on marriage and the family at California's Sonoma State College.

Among the couples who have sought his help, Dr. Pomeroy has found that conflicts usually stem from one partner wanting to participate while the other does not; a change in attitude since the original decision was made to participate, or, one of the partners becoming emotionally involved with a third person.

"If they are both interested and even enthusiastic about it [group sex], it's probably more beneficial in their marriage than detrimental," Dr. Pomeroy said:

When both partners are not interested or there is the threat of emotional involvement with a third person, Dr. Pomeroy endeavors "to get them to focus on the relationship in the marriage — on their own partner. The real issue is the marriage itself, not the extramarital affair."

Dr. Laura Singer, the president of the marriage counselor association's New York division, has also noted among her patients "increased participation in group sex or more willingness to discuss the subject."

"It's less of a detriment if they are open about it than if they are secretive, but I don't think it's not a detriment," she said. "I don't think it adds to the functioning of a marriage."

DR. SINGER SAID that involvement in group sex activities could, at times, be caused by fear of closeness.

"Underneath, there's a fear of getting terribly close to one person, and they can maintain a distance by diffused sexuality," she said.

For most of the men and women who have made a serious study of group sex, the practice is an indication of something missing, both in the participating individuals and in society.

"The fact that this is sexual may make it way out, but these people wholly reflect the imperatives of their society," said Dr. Gilbert D. Bartell, associate professor of anthropology at Northern Illinois University.

Dr. Bartell and his wife spent three years researching "Group Sex" (Peter H. Wyden, Inc., $6.95), a study of a selected sample of 280 suburban middleclass couples who participated in group sex in the Middle West. The book concentrates on the "organized swingers," a segment of the group sex scene that "lacks and fears emotional involvement."

These are the people who advertise in numerous publications available for the purpose, frequent certain cocktail lounges, go through standardized ritualistic procedures and were undoubtedly well represented in Chicago last summer among the 184 couples attending the First National Swingers Convention.

There are, however, at least two other types of participants in group sex.

The "Utopian swingers" are described as "concerned with building a better world ... they believe strongly in love and the physical expression of love."

The "recreational swingers" are men and women who believe "that it is more fun for people to have sex together than to play bridge and golf together, and who practice what they believe."

Marriage counselors, psychiatrists and sociologists are, for the most part, encountering participants in the recreational category, who usually live in large urban centers, and the organized swingers, who appear to be concentrated in suburban or more rural areas.

The young, when they participate (most studies appear to indicate that group sex is more attractive to men and women over 25), are inclined to be members of Utopian groups and apparently have fewer adjustments to make if and when they disassociate themselves from the concept.

Group sex was found to be "an emerging pattern of life in New York" in research done by Dr. George C. O'Neill and his wife, Nena, an anthropological team.

The O'Neills did not set out to study group sex but rather the problems of contemporary marriage. Their book, "Open Marriage, A New Lifestyle for Couples," to be published later this year by M. Evans, Inc., deals with ways of building a sound personal relationship.

Their suggestions do not include group sex, but their 50 in-depth interviews and 200 informal discussions with Manhattan group-sex participants left them with "general and tentative" impressions on respondents' reasons for participation.

Their sample comprised mainly middle-class business and professional people, spanning the occupational range from academe to the entertainment world. About 50 per cent had completed college. The majority were in the 30-to-50-year-old category, but single, married, divorced and widowed people were included. They found:

- Some of the married respondents were tired of cheating in extra-marital affairs but were not yet ready to grant their mate complete sexual autonomy.

- Some needed more sex than their spouse provided.

- Some felt restricted by marital exclusivity, and group sex provided a structured context in which to explore extramarital sex.

- Some were bored and restless and turned to group sex as a stimulant and sexual turn-on.

- Some were trying to patch up a failing marriage.

"It's probably going to be a fad — a phenomenon. For most people, nothing positive comes out of it because there is no deep bond between those involved," said Dr. O'Neill, professor of anthropology of the City College of New York.

Dr. O'Neill said that although other cultures have had forms of mate exchange and that sexual orgies were not unknown in Roman and Greek civilizations, to his knowledge, "in other cultures today, group sex does not occur the way it does here."

Both the O'Neills and Dr. Bartell agree that modern birth control methods probably contribute to the practice of group sex. They have, however, reservations about the impact of pornography, often quoted as another contributing factor.

"In our sample, I don't think pornography contributed," Mrs. O'Neill said. "It was general sexual permissiveness and the need for people to look outside for something because they were so deficient in their own relationship."

A YOUNG MARRIED COUPLE, who have engaged in group sex for the last year, disagree.

"I think we have an ideal marriage," said Mimi Lobell, a 28-year-old architectural designer. Her husband, John, 29, nodded agreement.

"It would be irresponsible for us to proselytize and tell everyone it's great," said Mrs. Lobell, who was brought up in Illinois and Indiana and was graduated from the University of Pennsylvania architectural school. "It wouldn't work for some people but it can work, and it doesn't have to dissolve a marriage."

The Lobells, who have been married five years, talked about group sex as "a possibility" for some years before they became active in it.

"We don't go out looking for people to have sex with," Mrs. Lobell said. "It's usually with people we've known awhile."

Mr. Lobell, a teacher at Pratt, described group sex as "an art form."

"It's life art," he explained. "Even though we are married, we are growing as people, and marriage should have to do with spiritual growth, not sexual exclusivity."

The Lobells, who engage in "one-to-one" affairs as well as in group sex, admit to "some jealousy."

"We do get jealous," Mr. Lobell said. "But it's about things we are insecure about. We are secure about sex and our relationship together so we don't get jealous about that, but if a guy takes Mimi out to an expensive restaurant, I might get jealous because I can't."

Mrs. Lobell's parents (her father is well-known educator) were informed of their daughter and son-in-law's activities only within the last month. According to Mr. Lobell, "Mimi's father said, 'I guess that's the younger generation,' and her mother said she was proud of us for speaking out for what we believe in."

Mr. Lobell's parents were told some time ago.

"My father was a Jewish boy from the Bronx who ran away to Greenwich Village to be an artist and then went back to study law," he said. "He's interested in what we are doing. My mother read Shaw before she went to school ... she's objective."

The Lobells agreed that if they had children, they "wouldn't hide anything" (studies of organized swingers indicated that they were inclined to skirt the issue but often set up one standard for themselves and another for their children).

"There is nothing inherent in sex that would scare or traumatize children to see it," Mr. Lobell said.

Dr. Lawrence Flatterer, a psychoanalyst, pointed out, however, that "nobody is living in a vacuum. A child brought up in such circumstances would be in for some kind of a problem unless the culture institutionalizes this practice."

Betty Dodson, a 41-year-old artist whose erotic paintings were given a one-woman show at the Wickersham Gallery in 1969, is another group sex participant who has no hesitation about admitting it.

"When I got divorced in 1965, I decided to find out everything I could about sexuality," she said. "I set about letting go of jealousy and possessive feelings, and understanding I could love more than one person. It was the most important thing I ever did."

Miss Dodson, who said she was married to an advertising executive and described her married life as "typical of that scene," said she no longer used the word "love."

"The essential problem is to learn how to be loving," she said. "Loving is an attitude."

Miss Dodson said she had found out, very quickly, that "group sex is something you do with friends."

"Organized group sex is a little bowling league kind of thing," she said. "It's super-compulsive — there's a frantic quality to it. It's weird."

SINCE HER INTRODUCTION to group sex, she has had both homosexual and heterosexual experiences (almost every study reports a high incidence of homosexual activity among females and very little homosexual activity among males).

"If you aren't into a sexual exchange that is bisexual, you aren't into sexual freedom," she said.

The statement was disputed by Dr. Hatterer, who commented: "That is imposing her notion on other people. The bulk of the population thinks of free heterosexual sex as the most liberated."

Dr. Bartell's study of organized group sex left him with the impression that "it doesn't hurt people in a social sense — they are out of the house, they are not living in suburban loneliness and isolation." He said, however, that it could have a deleterious psychological, effect.

He said that men, who most often initiated the idea of participating in group sex, might find that their fantasies were not being lived out. (Studies indicate that many women are initially negative to the idea of participating and sometimes go along because they are told their husbands will go elsewhere if they do not.)

The Bartell sampling was of women who discussed houses and children "and took great pride in the neatness and cleanliness of their homes" and of men who talked of taxes and sports, were antagonistic to some minority groups and strongly anti-hippie. The sampling also noted that although the majority did not attend church regularly, no one would admit to atheism or agnosticism and 85 per cent were giving their children some religious training.

Religion plays no part in the lives of the Lobells or Miss Dodson. Mr. Lobell said he was given no formal religious training; Mrs. Lobell, who was brought up a Protestant, said she had gone to church and Sunday school. Miss Dodson, the child of "nonreligious Protestant parents," said that, as a youngster, she had been baptized a Methodist at her own request.

"But," she continued, "organized religion is no longer a viable thing in our society. They are just not with it. They are too steeped in restrictions. You might say I am anti-organized religion and very much for inner spiritual development."

For Rabbi Irving Greenberg of the Riverdale Jewish Center, group sex "and the search for Utopian fulfillment" is a disintegrating force.

It is a breakdown of the capacity to live within limits and frustrations," said Rabbi Greenberg, who is a teacher at Yeshiva University. "It begins to destroy the reality."

"The ultimate fulfillment is to know one person totally," he added. "I admit it is difficult to do, but you cannot do it running from one to the other."

Group sex could be described as "a new form of prostitution," according to Father Charles E. Curran, professor at the School of Theology, Catholic University of America.

"One doesn't give oneself as a person, one gives just the body," he commented.

"The willingness to commit oneself to another over a period of time is important. What this whole thing brings to mind is the future of the family and parenthood ... . I still think the family is a necessary part of society."

The Rev. Dr. Joseph Fletcher, professor of medical ethics at the School of Medicine, University of Virginia, said "it [group sex] might be distasteful to me, but I couldn't hold it immoral."

"In my understanding of ethics, nothing is ever right or wrong in itself and regardless of circumstances, and that applies to the Ten Commandments as well," said Dr. Fletcher, who for 27 years was Professor of Social Ethics at the Episcopal Theological School in Cambridge, Mass.

DR. BARTELL'S CONCLUSION after his survey was that although group sex is apparently growing, it will diminish "as college kids come of age."

"I don't think they have the same approach to sex as their parents," he said. "They participate earlier, experiment more freely. The earlier experience may be advantageous to them because later they may want to establish a good human relationship, rather than simply a sexual one."

"The kids are back to romance," said Dr. Hatterer. "If they do something like this, it's for kicks. Many of them call this a 'freak scene.' "

He cited rebellion against high restraints and inhibitions, inability to establish one-to-one relationships, fear of being committed to an intimate relationship and poor sex education as some of the possible reasons for current interest.

"New sexual patterns of behavior have entered and become more acceptable in our culture," he said. "They bring wider hedonistic horizons. We don't really know what the fallout will be in such situations.

"I'll put my money on it. The next cycle will be sex addiction — people who do things compulsively, not because they are having a good time and expressing affection, but because they will use excesses in sex to deal with nonsexual matters, like failure, competition and anxiety.

"The only way to deal with it will be a sound, open and good sex education program. Some of the most sophisticated parents don't talk to their children about sex."

Sexuality and Other Female (Film) Troubles

BY JULIE BLOOM | MAY 11, 2012

"THE PLAGUE OF OUR TIMES," a character declares in "Hysteria," Tanya Wexler's new romantic comedy about the invention of the vibrator in Victorian England, "stems from an overactive uterus." Based loosely on real events and opening on Friday, the film stars Hugh Dancy as Mortimer, a charming, forward-thinking doctor, and Maggie Gyllenhaal as Charlotte, a champion of women's rights.

Though its period detail and depiction of naïve men trying to "cure" hysterical women through pelvic massage seems hilariously out of date, there are moments when issues of women's rights raised (lightly) in the film feel surprisingly relevant. But more than anything, "Hysteria" serves as a reminder that female sexuality is still an unusual subject on screen.

There are signs, however, that this may be changing. "Girls" on HBO has attracted attention for its frank depiction of sex, and Lena Dunham's role as a show runner gives her rare authority to depict sexuality from a woman's perspective. It's a role that's equally rare in film: female directors accounted for just 5 percent of the top-grossing domestic movies last year, a report from the Center for the Study of Women in Television and Film found.

New and recent films by Ms. Wexler, Sarah Polley ("Take This Waltz"), Malgorzata Szumowska ("Elles"), Julie Delpy ("2 Days in New York") and several others challenge this norm and give audiences the chance to see how women deal with issues of female sexuality, whether it's orgasms or body image.

"I wanted to make a Merchant-Ivory movie with vibrators," Ms. Wexler, 42, said sitting in an office in Midtown Manhattan, her long brown hair bouncing every time she let out a booming laugh. "And in doing that, strangely, we've shone a light. Can you believe we're still

Director Tanya Wexler.

arguing about these same topics 100 years later — women's rights over their own body? If a woman is behind the camera, these issues can be explored more than they have in the past."

Still, "I just wanted a movie I wanted to go see," she added. "I wasn't trying to do a women's studies class."

Ms. Wexler's own experiences informed the humorous — and chaste — treatment scenes, in which women of different ages are "cured." For instance she recalled the situation many women find themselves in at the gynecologist's office, feet in stirrups while doctors chitchat. "You're like, 'Dude I'm sitting here,' " she said.

Working from a script by the husband-and-wife team Stephen Dyer and Jonah Lisa Dyer, Ms. Wexler spent close to seven years working to get the film made with the producer Tracey Becker, who said it was not an easy sell. "We saw the marketing potential," Ms. Becker said, "but when it came right down to it, we had this script which dealt with these very blush-inducing themes, and most of the time it was in the hands of a male executive, who had the veto power."

"Hysteria" represents something of a departure from the traditional studio film aimed at women, and Ms. Wexler, Ms. Polley and others said there was a hunger for more movies that don't just end with a kiss and marriage.

"I like a good wedding-dress movie, like all girls, if they're good," Ms. Wexler said, "but it's just not all we want."

Ms. Polley's "Take This Waltz," which will be released next month, starts a few years after the wedding, with Michelle Williams as a young married woman confronting temptation. "I wanted to look at what happens to sexuality over time, and it's something we don't talk about," Ms. Polley said in a telephone interview.

In part because men have been in the director's seat, "the cliché is always the woman has a headache or is tired of sex, or there's some kind of burning out of sexuality, and I couldn't remember an example of the opposite — that men get bored and men have a dropping-off of sexual intensity too," Ms. Polley said. "Maybe men don't show that because it's emasculating, but it does happen to men in long-term relationships."

Nudity, Ms. Polley said, was also important for her to address as a director. "Every time you see a naked woman's body on screen, it's either in a sexual context — or if it's an older woman it's the scene in 'About Schmidt,' where Kathy Bates gets in to the hot tub and the whole audience is supposed to scream, and Jack Nicholson is so horrified," she said. "I've seen that over and over, and I find that really offensive that women's bodies are either objectified or used for comic value."

In "Take This Waltz" Ms. Polley included a shower scene in a health club with women of all ages naked in a completely casual way. "That scene came specifically out of being a female filmmaker," she said, "I would have maybe pretended a few years ago that I just want to make stories like everyone else, and my gender didn't matter, but I think that's naïve. Certainly with this film I was very conscious of the way I was handling nudity and sexuality."

For actresses, having a female director can influence the dynamic during sex scenes. Ms. Gyllenhaal said that a female director changes the feel of a film. "The most interesting sex scenes that I've done or seen are the ones that are truthful from a women's perspective," she said. "Instead of what I think everybody got used to in the '80s and '90s: Put on a black Victoria's Secret demi bra and be lit perfectly and arch your back."

"That's supposed to look like sex," she added, "but that doesn't look like sex for most people, and if it does, I think you're probably missing out on a lot."

Juliette Binoche, who stars in "Elles," Ms. Szumowska's graphic look at student prostitutes in Paris that was released last month, also noticed the difference a female director makes. "Because I'm used to working with male directors, working with a woman there was a new feeling I had which was related to something more personal, it felt like an auto-portrait at some moments," she said. "And so the responsibility of acting with a director of the same sex, it's something of a mirroring feeling."

Ms. Wexler and her colleagues said that making movies that focus on female sexuality also meant risking being pigeonholed as a director only for women. Noting that Marc Webb followed up the romantic comedy "(500) Days of Summer" with "The Amazing Spider-Man," Ms. Wexler said: "I doubt that I'm getting 'The Avengers' or 'Justice League.' I want to do movies for women, but I don't only want to do that."

For Ms. Wexler, and others, more films by women about women is no doubt progress, but, she added, that inevitably presents another set of challenges. "What we're doing as women by making these small, little movies, because that's all they'll give us, is we're making things that don't make as much money, that have a smaller audience and are harder to get right, and then we're wondering why we don't get bigger movies. That is very self-reinforcing. I would love me a big Hollywood movie. 'Wonder Woman'? Give me a call."

Tinder, the Fast-Growing Dating App, Taps an Age-Old Truth

BY NICK BILTON | OCT. 29, 2014

WEST HOLLYWOOD, CALIF. — As I sat in the lobby of a drab office building here, waiting to be led up to the penthouse loft of Tinder, the fast-growing dating app, I noticed that every few minutes young women would walk into the foyer, dressed in flip-flops, T-shirts and tattered jean shorts, and then go through a radical transformation.

Swapping out their rubber sandals for stiletto heels, they smeared on globs of lip gloss and flung on leather jackets. After a 30-second wardrobe change, they were ready for their appointments at a modeling agency on the ground floor. Same people: two very different personas.

A short elevator ride later, as I sat in on a meeting with a group of Tinder executives, it became clear that the quick-change act I had just witnessed downstairs, though unrelated to Tinder, still had a lot to do with what was going on upstairs. What someone wears, along with other visual clues given off in photographs, can tell a thousand different things about them.

And Tinder believes that these clues are the key to online dating.

In the two years since Tinder was released, the smartphone app has exploded, processing more than a billion swipes left and right daily (right means you "like" someone, left means you don't) and matching more than 12 million people in that same time, the company said. Tinder wouldn't share the exact number of people on the service, saying only that it was on par with other social networks at two years in operation. But a person with knowledge of the situation told me that it is fast approaching 50 million active users.

Tinder's engagement is staggering. The company said that, on average, people log into the app 11 times a day. Women spend as much as 8.5 minutes swiping left and right during a single session; men spend 7.2 minutes. All of this can add up to 90 minutes each day.

While conventional online dating sites have been around longer, they haven't come close to the popularity of Tinder. Scientists and relationship specialists who study online dating suggest it isn't what Tinder is doing correctly, but rather what earlier dating sites have done wrong.

Services like eHarmony, OKCupid and Match.com have proclaimed that their proprietary algorithms could calculate true love, or that math equations could somehow pluck two strangers to live happily ever after. That appears to be more fiction than fact.

All that really matters, according to scientific researchers I spoke with from Northwestern University and Illinois State University, at least in the beginning of relationship, is how someone looks. (Of course, these companies disagree.)

Before you throw your hands in the air and proclaim that such a statement is indicative of today's degenerating society, what's happening on Tinder is actually a lot more complicated.

"When was the last time you walked into a bar and someone said, 'Excuse me, can you fill out this form and we'll match you up with people here?' " said Sean Rad, co-founder and chief executive of Tinder, referring to the questionnaires on most dating sites. "That's not how we think about meeting new people in real life."

On Tinder, there are no questionnaires to fill out. No discussion of your favorite hiking trail, star sign or sexual proclivities. You simply log in through Facebook, pick a few photos that best describe "you" and start swiping.

It may seem that what happens next is predictable (the best-looking people draw the most likes, the rest are quickly dismissed), but relationship experts for Tinder say there is something entirely different going on.

"Research shows when people are evaluating photos of others, they are trying to access compatibility on not just a physical level, but a social level," said Jessica Carbino, Tinder's in-house dating and relationship expert. "They are trying to understand, 'Do I have things in common with this person?' "

Ms. Carbino, who recently concluded a Ph.D. candidacy at the University of California, Los Angeles, where she focused her research on dating, romantic relationships and what men and women are drawn to when evaluating a partner, joined Tinder this summer to help the company understand what kind of visual cues could cause a person to swipe "like" or "nope."

She discovered that Tinder users decoded an array of subtle and not-so-subtle traits before deciding which way to swipe. For example, the style of clothing, the pucker of the lips and even the posture, Ms. Carbino said, tell us a lot about their social circle, if they like to party and their level of confidence.

Tinder also conducted studies to try to glean more insight into users' behaviors. In one survey, women were asked to swipe through a series of photos of handsome male models. In almost every instance, the women swiped to the left, dismissing the men with chiseled faces. When asked why, the women said that the men looked too full of themselves or unkind. "Men with softer jaw lines indicate that they have more compassion," Ms. Carbino said.

Men also judge attractiveness on factors beyond just anatomy, though in general, men are nearly three times as likely to swipe "like" (in 46 percent of cases) than woman (14 percent).

"There is this idea that attraction stems from a very superficial outlook on people, which is false," Mr. Rad said. "Everyone is able to pick up thousands of signals in these photos. A photo of a guy at a bar with friends around him sends a very different message than a photo of a guy with a dog on the beach."

Digital dating services are far from new. Computerized matchmaking sprang up in the mid-1960s, promising computer-guided mathematical equations that would help people find true love with a sprinkle of ones and zeros. "For $3 to $6 apiece, the computer-pairers promise to come up with the names — and addresses or telephone numbers — of 3 to 14, or even 100, ideal mates-dates," noted a 1966 article in The Toledo Blade, describing a Tinder-like predecessor called, "Pick 'em cuter by computer."

Yet since those days, while computers have become incalculably smarter, the ability of machines and algorithms to match people has remained just as clueless in the view of independent scientists.

"We, as a scientific community, do not believe that these algorithms work," said Eli J. Finkel, an associate professor of social psychology at Northwestern University. To him, dating sites like eHarmony and Match.com are more like modern snake oil. "They are a joke, and there is no relationship scientist that takes them seriously as relationship science."

Conventional dating sites dispute this. In a statement, eHarmony acknowledged that its algorithms are proprietary, but said that its methods have been tested by academic experts. The company also scoffed at Mr. Finkel's claims, saying his views are not part of "meaningful discussions that can be had about how compatibility can be measured and predicted." Match.com did not respond to a request for comment.

Mr. Finkel worked for more than a year with a group of researchers trying to understand how these algorithm-based dating services could match people, as they claim to do. The team pored through more than 80 years of scientific research about dating and attraction, and was unable to prove that computers can indeed match people together.

While companies like eHarmony still assert they have a "scientific approach" to helping people fall in love, some dating sites are starting to acknowledge that the only thing that matters when matching lovers is someone's picture. Earlier this year, OKCupid examined its data and found that a person's profile picture is, said a post on its Oktrends blog, "worth that fabled thousand words, but your actual words are worth... almost nothing."

But this doesn't mean that the most attractive people are the only ones who find true love. Indeed, in many respects, it can be the other way around.

Earlier this year Paul W. Eastwick, an assistant professor of human development and family sciences at the University of Texas at Austin, and Lucy L. Hunt, a graduate student, published a paper noting that a person's unique looks are what is most important when trying to find a mate. "There isn't a consensus about who is attractive and who isn't," Mr. Eastwick said in an interview. "Someone that you think is especially attractive might not be to me. That's true with photos, too." Tinder's data team echoed this, noting that there isn't a cliquey, high school mentality on the site, where one group of users gets the share of "like" swipes.

While Tinder seems to have done a lot of things right, the company has also made plenty of mistakes. For example, some women have complained of being harassed on the service. The company has had its own sexual harassment issues inside the office. And all that swiping has given Tinder the nickname "the hookup app," for its reputation for one-night stands — though the company tries to distance itself from the label.

One thing is certain: Whether Tinder is used for a late-night rendezvous or for finding a soul mate lies just as much in the eye of the swiper as it does in the way people choose to represent themselves.

This was perfectly exemplified as I wrapped up another visit to Tinder's offices. As I walked out of the elevator into the lobby, I saw two women leaving the modeling agency. One paused, shedding her high heels and fancy jacket in lieu of flip-flops and T-shirt, while the other stayed in her glamorous outfit, walking outside as if she were strolling into a late-night club or onto a catwalk.

Same people: two very different personas.

Should 'Slut' Be Retired?

BY ANNA NORTH | FEB. 3, 2015

THE WORD "SLUT," says Leora Tanenbaum, has changed.

Once largely derogatory, she writes in her new book, "I Am Not a Slut: Slut-Shaming in the Age of the Internet," the word has become a way for girls and women themselves "to assert a positive, even defiant attitude about their sexuality." Ms. Tanenbaum believes this assertion is misplaced — the word "slut," she argues, is too dangerous to be reclaimed.

While not everyone sees the word "slut" the same way Ms. Tanenbaum does, many agree that girls and women today face intense and conflicting pressures when it comes to their sexuality. And to push back against those pressures, some say, they may need tools more complex and diverse than a single word.

Ms. Tanenbaum, who is also the senior writer and editor for the Planned Parenthood Federation of America, first wrote about the word "slut" in 1999. Since then, she says, limitations on women's sexuality have gotten only more complex. "Females are supposed to police themselves and to remain minimally sexual, but at the same time females also are not supposed to be prudes," Ms. Tanenbaum explained, "and I think that the presence of social media has really ramped up that contradictory pressure." Young women have long feared being labeled prudish, she said, "but it wasn't as oppressive as it is now."

In "I Am Not a Slut," she writes that for some teenage girls, "being a 'slut' is good — but only when the girl herself is orchestrating her reputation and maintains control over it." Being called a "slut" in some contexts can mean a girl is socially important — and, she writes, "in some social circles, it is compulsory to achieve 'good slut' status. A girl must behave like a 'good slut' whether she wants to or not." But "once a girl achieves 'good slut' status, she is always at risk of losing control and becoming known as a 'bad slut' " who is ostracized and shamed.

Jamia A. Wilson, a staff writer for Rookie, a website for teenage girls, and the executive director of the nonprofit Women, Action, and the Media, said she experienced some of these tensions when she was a teenager, "but I think it's gotten worse because of social media and texting."

"The same sort of things that were happening before, the shaming and the pressure, can happen to you in a much more quick, rapid, and viral way," she explained.

Nor do these pressures necessarily come only from boys and men. "Girls and young women are pressured to present themselves as these good sluts," said Ms. Tanenbaum, "but then when they do what they think they're supposed to be doing, so many other people, including women, including some feminists, will wag a finger in their faces."

In a recent essay at The New Inquiry, Anna Breslaw takes Tina Fey to task for her comments on other women's sexual behavior: Her " 'nerdy' on-screen persona and adamant faux feminism masks a Thatcherite morality and tendency to slut-shame," Ms. Breslaw writes. She also cites Ms. Fey's criticisms of the "other women" in high-profile extramarital affairs:

"Fey gives her support to the only women who she feels deserve it: 'Wives, you're not the losers in these situations. You are the winners.'

" 'Winning' in Tina Fey's playbook means being immensely attractive but safe from being marginalized thanks to a smart sense of self-deprecation as well as the compulsion to slam other women who don't feel the need to sublimate their looks or their sexuality."

"The punishment of women for their sexuality is so deeply ingrained in our culture that I don't think any facet escapes it," Melissa Febos, the author of "Whip Smart," a memoir of her time as a dominatrix, said in an interview. "As a woman who has always embodied disparate qualities (at least by social prescriptions of femininity), I have been policed my whole life. As a feminist/intellectual/queer I can't do a lot of things — be a sex worker, wear makeup and heels, be bisexual, watch pornography, go on a diet, and so forth."

"I've been told in myriad ways that I can't have it all ways," she added. "Only in my 30s have I stopped worrying the problem. It's not my problem to work out." Still, she said, "it pains and frustrates me to see this kind of judging and conflict within feminist communities."

Feminism has long dealt with tension over women's self-presentation, said Sady Doyle, a writer on gender and culture whose critique of Tina Fey's Liz Lemon character on the sitcom "30 Rock" is oft-cited, including by Ms. Breslaw. In the 1970s, many feminists pushed back against the expectation that they appear sexually attractive in a traditionally feminine way at all times: "A lot of that early resistance was about, 'we don't want to have to present ourselves in sexualized ways. We want to be able to just show up in pantsuits, or in T-shirts and jeans, and be able to be processed as people.' " At the same time, a rejection of the traditionally feminine can feed into "the idea that is ingrained in us by the patriarchy that we are always in competition with other women, that if a woman is presenting herself as sexual and it's really working out for her, she's sort of selling the rest of us out, or she's selling herself out."

"It's so tempting to sort of assume," she said, that "a presentation that's not traditionally sexy and feminine means there's substance there, and a presentation that is really sexy and feminine just means that you care about what boys think." But that kind of assumption is damaging, she argued: "It's a way for women to delegitimize each other, and ultimately it allows men to delegitimize both sets."

And Ms. Wilson cites Bell Hooks's criticism of Beyoncé's Time magazine cover as an example of intra-feminist judgment: "I remember being really heartbroken" by Dr. Hooks's comments, she said. "That was really, really problematic for me because these are both women who I see as feminist role models, and who have helped inform my feminism as young woman of color," Ms. Wilson added. The incident "was a perfect example of what work we need to be doing within our communities to have these conversations in a way that we don't undermine and subjugate each other."

SlutWalk protests arose as one response to the judgment of women's clothing choices and perceived sexual behavior. They became popular in 2011, Ms. Tanenbaum notes, in part precipitated by a Toronto police officer's comment that "women should avoid dressing like sluts in order not to be victimized." But reclamation of the word has seemed less helpful to some than to others. Ms. Tanenbaum writes that racism is baked into the history of the word: In centuries past, it wasn't used to refer to black women, because "black women were regarded as inherently slutty, unlike white women, whose sluttiness represented a supposed transgression of true femininity."

And, she adds, the organization Black Women's Blueprint took issue with SlutWalk in an open letter arguing that "as Black women, we do not have the privilege or the space to call ourselves 'slut' without validating the already historically entrenched ideology and recurring messages about what and who the Black woman is."

"We acknowledged, and we in fact very, very much agreed that there should not be slut-shaming," Farah Tanis, the executive director of Black Women's Blueprint, said in an interview. But, she explained, black women's "relationship to the term 'slut' " is informed by a history of racism and slavery, of "having been seen as objects of property, not just for the sexual gratification of those in power but also for reproduction of whole generations of slaves, which involved rape most of the time." It's informed, too, by the racist stereotype of the Jezebel: "The Jezebel was a predator, and the Jezebel was insatiable, and the Jezebel could never be raped."

"What the word 'slut' conjures up for us is these ancestral narratives and experiences that have been passed down," she said.

"As an African-American woman who grew up in mostly white environments," Ms. Wilson said, she found discussions of the word "slut" personally helpful, "because that was a term that was being lobbed in the communities I was in." But for those who didn't grow up in such environments, she said, discussions of the term may not feel as relevant. "When we think about reclaiming of our bodies on our own terms," she said, "that's what makes sense to me. So if it makes sense to say 'slut-shaming' because that is your truth and how you've lived it, that's perfectly valid." Others may prefer to talk about "body-shaming as it relates to race or class" in ways the word "slut" doesn't capture.

"The word itself is a terrible word," she added, "but it's not necessarily the focus. It's actually the root causes that are the problem that we should all be working on."

"If people really put their minds to it," Ms. Tanis said, "they could probably reclaim the word 'slut.' But for me I wouldn't want to, because reclaiming means that it was yours in the first place." And the word "slut" is "not something that I created for myself, it's something that was created for a particular purpose, and the purpose wasn't to serve me."

What she'd like to see is more criticism of media representations of women and their sexuality — more resistance to films in which women depicted as "slutty" "are the ones that get raped first, or the ones that get killed first, thereby implanting this idea that these are the women that are worthless." She also believes in the efficacy of marching for social change — but she said, the SlutWalk marches "could have been so much bigger and so much more productive if everyone had a particular message that they were expounding based on the experiences of their race, their culture, their class, their gender identity, their sexuality. I think that this was a moment to unite us all, because we all have an issue with slut-shaming. And I think it's a moment that was missed."

Ms. Tanenbaum, for her part, believes the word "slut" should be retired — at least for now. "Maybe in the future, we will be at a point where we can use the word 'slut' as an ironic in-joke, as a feminist punch line, as a badge of honor," she said, "and I hope we do." But, she said, "the problem is that for most people in the United States, the word 'slut' means 'shameful, disgusting woman who's out of control sexually, and needs to be put in her place and deserves to have bad things happen to her, including being sexually assaulted.' For that reason, I think it is too risky right now to use that word."

To mitigate the pressures she sees facing girls and women, Ms. Tanenbaum calls for "comprehensive sex education, birth control without interference from politicians and bosses and abortion without judgment."

"Those are concrete, material things that need to happen to destigmatize female sexuality," she said, "and I think if we destigmatize female sexuality we will diminish the culture of slut-shaming and slut-bashing."

Ms. Doyle believes that combating stereotypes about women who present themselves as sexy in a certain way "is a continual process. It's unlearning."

"I think it's about bringing the assumptions into the light, it's about talking through them openly, and it's about acknowledging that any set of ideas about women that's this old and this pervasive is going to crop up for you time and time again," she said, "and you have to be prepared to face it and work it through."

For Ms. Wilson, disagreements among feminists about women's self-presentation require "really thinking about, how do we talk about each other and our work and critique each other" without "rendering the other person as disposable."

"How do we talk about places where we're different in the work without undermining everyone's ideas?" she asked. "It's really about having these conversations in a way that there's an openness, and also in a way that there's a respect that is missing a lot of the time when this happens."

Ms. Wilson said that Jaclyn Friedman and Jessica Valenti's book "Yes Means Yes!: Visions of Female Sexual Power and a World Without Rape" "really gave me a lot of those answers about how do we define healthy sexuality for ourselves, and how do we do it without shame." The phrase "yes means yes," she noted, has "caught on" — new California legislation often called the " 'yes means yes' law" defines consent as "an affirmative, conscious and voluntary agreement to engage in sexual activity," rather than simply the absence of a "no."

The "yes means yes" formulation "comes from a place of sexual power, rather than one of subjugation," she said. In that spirit, young women can ask themselves: "What makes you feel powerful? What makes you feel in control of your body and yourself? What feels safe for you?"

"Real sexual freedom for a woman would be about defining your idea of what great sex is from a really subjective personal view-point," said Ms. Doyle. We'll achieve it "when we recognize sex is an incredibly individual, weird thing, everybody experiences it a little differently, everybody wants something a little bit different, every-body communicates it in their presentation a little bit differently than everybody else."

"Dropping the self-consciousness and being free to process what is most fulfilling for you without being afraid that someone else is going to come in and tear your life down or not give you a job or not promote you at your job or socially exclude you," she said. "That would be the utopia."

How Hugh Hefner
Invented the Modern Man

OPINION | BY AMBER BATURA | SEPT. 28, 2017

LUBBOCK, TEX. — In December 1953, the inaugural issue of Playboy magazine hit newsstands without a date. Hugh Hefner, its creator, was unsure whether it would be a success and have a future, so by withholding the date he hoped he could continue to sell that issue until he sold out of that first run.

Mr. Hefner, who died on Wednesday at 91, had nothing to worry about.

In its prime, the magazine ranked among America's top-selling publications, alongside Life and Time, sometimes beating their subscription rates. The magazine, intended for men, quickly transcended Mr. Hefner's target audience, with a subscriber base that cut across gender, race, class and ideology.

Today it's easy to write off Playboy, and Mr. Hefner, as the last remnants of a more sexist age. But seen from the perspective of the 1950s and '60s, they were progressive icons — not just in the libertine styles they promoted, but in the causes that they featured. The magazine became central to what it meant to be a modern man.

The masculine ideal of the era was narrowly defined: aloof, outdoorsy, a breadwinner, "manly." Showing too much of an interest in culture, fine food or travel was anathema. Mr. Hefner felt trapped by conformity and designed a magazine that promoted a very different idea of what made an individual a "man" through its features and advice on clothing, food, alcohol selections, art, music and literature. Though it quickly became a cliché, many male readers really did "read it for the articles," telling surveys that they enjoyed features on the ideal bachelor pad even more than the centerfold.

Of course, Playboy was never just about the articles. From the beginning, its goal was to combine and appeal to men's entire range of interests — the intellectual, the entertaining and the erotic. Hence the Playboy Playmate, which Mr. Hefner modeled after Esquire's Vargas Girls, popular among servicemen during World War II. Women in the magazine, he said, were intended more as the girl next door than as sex objects.

Still, the fact that they were often topless (full nudity didn't appear until 1972) brought criticism that Mr. Hefner objectified women; promoted an unrealistic standard of female beauty; and promulgated the idea that women should be subservient playmates for the modern man. To Mr. Hefner, women were simply one of the interests of most heterosexual men. The magazine featured discussions of equal rights, contraception and reproductive choice. Mr. Hefner never saw that as a contradiction.

As the magazine's editorial style evolved, Mr. Hefner and his editors delved more into politics and current events. By the 1960s, he was writing a frequent installment, "The Playboy Philosophy," in which he addressed topics like the First Amendment and sexual mores. He advocated gay rights. He pushed for women's access to birth control and abortion. He discussed censorship as well as what constituted "obscene" in the United States, and he promoted the free exchange of thoughts and ideas.

And readers responded. So many wrote in that the magazine created "The Playboy Forum," where it published readers' letters discussing the content of the "Philosophy." Playboy became more than just a magazine, but a place that facilitated dialogue among a wide variety of readers: Men, women, veterans, draft dodgers, congressmen and clergy all wrote into the Forum.

Mr. Hefner went beyond the pages of Playboy to spread his message. He created the Playboy Club franchise to bring the atmosphere of the magazine to life for its readers. They could buy good food, good liquor and good entertainment.

He integrated his staff and membership; he hired men and women of all races, and often provided black comedians and musicians their first chances to perform in front of white audiences. When a New Orleans and Miami club owner segregated the membership, Mr. Hefner bought those franchises back. The clubs provided female employees with tuition reimbursement and encouraged them to attend college.

Mr. Hefner also set up the Playboy Foundation, which supported First Amendment rights, often contributing to defendants in free-speech cases. The foundation went on to support other works, including research on post-traumatic stress disorder, commissions on Agent Orange and programs and organizations for veterans.

Those latter causes were no coincidence: Playboy played a major role in the American war in Vietnam. For hundreds of thousands of young men "in country" — their average age was 19 — the magazine made them feel as if they were back home. The centerfold pages hung on tent flaps and office walls, and could be found stashed in pockets, helmets and packs. The interest went beyond the women: Young soldiers eagerly perused the glossy advertisements for the latest stereos, cars and fashion, which they could buy at one of the mall-like PXs on the military's sprawling bases (yes, even cars, which the government would ship home). It acted as a how-to guide for consumption and consumerism for many young men who had never had disposable income before.

Articles and interviews in the magazine were some of their only sources of real news about the growing antiwar and counterculture movements stateside. They went beyond the headlines, too, discussing and critiquing strategy, the draft and the politicians who moved the chess pieces. But the magazine also remained supportive of the men fighting the war. Countless letters from servicemen to the magazine, now stored in the Playboy archives, reveal how much the magazine lifted morale, how it brought a welcome respite from the boredom, terror and chaos they endured on a daily basis.

While the magazine deserved criticism, its evolution reflected changing norms and values in American society.

In August 1967, a soldier named Donald Iasillo wrote to Playboy thanking the magazine for literally saving his life. An issue folded in his chest pocket had prevented a bullet from entering his heart. "Usually for reasons other than its value as armor plate, Playboy is by far the biggest morale booster in Vietnam," he wrote. "For this, we all thank you."

AMBER BATURA is a doctoral candidate in history at Texas Tech University.

The Feminist Pursuit of Good Sex

OPINION | BY NONA WILLIS ARONOWITZ | FEB. 16, 2018

IN MY JUNIOR YEAR of college, before I'd learned much about feminism, I became fascinated by what we now call the 1970s "golden era" of pornography. Porno chic! Clitoral orgasms! A little film called "Deep Throat"! Being a lusty, modern woman, I was enthralled. I resolved to write my senior thesis on the role of that period in changing sexual mores.

And then, pretty quickly, I was confused. Was pornography a vanguard of sexual freedom or a tool of the patriarchy? Caught in a dizzying tangle of opinions from Second Wave feminist writers, many of whom were deeply ambivalent about the fruits of the sexual revolution, I sought guidance from my mother, the journalist and critic Ellen Willis, who in a 1981 essay in The Village Voice asked a question that now looms over #MeToo 40 years later: "Is the Women's Movement Pro-Sex?"

She enlightened me to a strain of early radical feminism that would forever change my thinking on the importance of pleasure politics. Both pornography and men could be misogynistic and predatory, she told me. But they weren't the causes so much as the symptoms of a sexist society. And the answer wasn't sexual repression. Women's liberation should not be "about fending off men's sexuality," she said, "but being able to embrace your own."

My connection to this complex intellectual heritage is at the heart of why I find the prevailing narrative about #MeToo's generational split baffling and harmful. Here's how the story goes: Older critics, flattened into "Second Wave feminist has-beens," are accusing the movement of becoming increasingly anti-sex, anti-agency and anti-nuance. Younger women, also known as "Twitter feminists," are accusing these critics of being bitter establishmentarians, unable to cede ground to new ideas. They're both wrong, but so is this tired mothers-and-daughters framing, which threatens to derail substantive debate in favor of a catfight narrative.

There are real reasons younger and older women may be experiencing this moment differently. To the extent that there is a generational divide, it may reflect many older women's wariness of the internet, which leads them to not only miss the context of a feminist internet tradition of ironic misandry but also to overlook the more nuanced chatter happening among younger women on social media and digital sites.

Second Wave feminism's reputation, meanwhile, as a humorless group of mainstream white women is due partly to a deliberate attempt in the 1980s to disparage feminists, but also to the movement's race and class blind spots. Add that to a perennial pastime of hating on that nebulous group called millennials and we have the makings of what, on the surface, can be read as a generational feud.

And yet most of the disagreement has to do with ideas about sex, power and the function of social movements — disputes that have divided feminists for decades.

There have always been liberal feminists, from Betty Friedan to Sheryl Sandberg, who wanted a seat at the table rather than to reset the table, who seek equal opportunity within existing power structures. They include older feminists, who endured pats on the bottom to succeed in the workplace and who urged the movement to prioritize things like women's economic empowerment rather than sexuality, which they considered frivolous and distracting. But there are younger feminists, too, who wish #MeToo would focus on predetermined bad behavior, like rape, rather than rethink tolerated behavior, like sexual pressure, and bristle at suggestions of a connection between the two.

And there have always been radical feminists, who want to see the system upended. In fact, the most famous radicals were Second Wave feminists, and some of their work provided the blueprint for #MeToo. Catharine MacKinnon was an early architect of sexual harassment's legal definition (and has publicly supported today's movement). Susan Brownmiller's book "Against Our Will" popularized the crucial concept of rape as power. Of course, this wing of radical feminism veered into cries of censorship and victimhood, endorsing a sexual moralism disturbingly similar to the religious right.

But what both activists and their critics are missing is that if #MeToo draws on the work of Ms. MacKinnon and Ms. Brownmiller, it's also rooted firmly in the tradition of the other radical Second Wavers. These women were absolutely pro-sex, pro-pleasure and pro-freedom. "We've got to learn to sleep with people because we want them," one woman said in a consciousness-raising session transcribed by the author of "The Dialectic of Sex," Shulamith Firestone, in 1968. "Not to prove anything to them, not to make them feel better about their masculinity, not out of weakness or inability to say no, but simply because we want to."

But they also understood that if rape and harassment were political, so was bad sex. In a 1980 essay, the radical feminist Alix Kates Shulman remembered that in those early sessions, "sex was a central and explosive subject to which we continually returned"; feminists "used their sexual discontents to help them understand the power relations between men and women."

I was reminded of this history when the website Babe published its Aziz Ansari article in January. The account of the so-called bad date, during which Mr. Ansari is alleged to have badgered a woman into going further than she wanted to, was an example of reckless reporting and was cited by many as #MeToo's too-far moment. But the instinct that it was an important article was correct. The issue of consensual yet joyless and unsatisfying sex was the same one my mom and her friends were grappling with 50 years ago.

At bottom, #MeToo is not about hashtags or individual firings. It's a chance to reset the table of sexual politics — not by infantilizing women or declaring a war on flirting or administering litmus tests, but by continuing a decades-long push for true equality in the bedroom, for a world in which women are not intimidated or coerced into sex but are also not stuffed into the role of gatekeepers.

For such a movement, the history of Second Wave pro-sex feminism should serve as both North Star and cautionary tale. Ultimately, the arguments of these women got swallowed up by the more coherent, consistent narrative of sexual conservatism, and later by a largely depoliticized version of pro-sex feminism that presented hot-pink dildos as the key to liberation. One reason this might have happened is that amid these conversations, men were at best ancillary and at worst demonized, an understandable impulse in the 1970s, when the most basic feminist ideas were scary and radical. "A free woman needs a free man," a woman said in a rare moment of clarity during that same 1968 consciousness-raising session.

But there may be a deeper reason this history has been obscured. In a 1982 essay, my mother admits that a misstep of the early pro-sex feminists was "the failure to put forward a convincing alternative analysis of sexual violence, exploitation and alienation."

The burgeoning movement, in other words, didn't make a compelling enough argument for freeing women's sexuality rather than tamping down men's, a distinction that makes clear the connection between bad sex and rape culture, between Harvey Weinstein's monster and Aziz Ansari's Everyman. Instead, just a few years later, protection from violence became the narrow, defensive definition of feminist sexual politics, and the concept of pleasure became synonymous with narcissism and self-indulgence.

This is the time to rectify all that. Condemning a culture that excuses sexual assault and harassment isn't about weakness and victimhood. It's about what my mom, who died in 2006, scrawled on a pamphlet from the famous 1982 Barnard Conference on Sexuality, which she mailed to me while I was toiling on my thesis. On it, she'd written this plain but transformative note: "Feminism is a vision of active freedom, of fulfilled desires, or it is nothing."

NONA WILLIS ARONOWITZ is the features editor at Splinter.

The Redistribution of Sex

OPINION | BY ROSS DOUTHAT | MAY 2, 2018

ONE LESSON TO BE DRAWN from recent Western history might be this: Sometimes the extremists and radicals and weirdos see the world more clearly than the respectable and moderate and sane. All kinds of phenomena, starting as far back as the Iraq War and the crisis of the euro but accelerating in the age of populism, have made more sense in the light of analysis by reactionaries and radicals than as portrayed in the organs of establishment opinion.

This is part of why there's been so much recent agitation over universities and op-ed pages and other forums for debate. There's a general understanding that the ideological mainstream isn't adequate to the moment, but nobody can decide whether that means we need purges or pluralism, a spirit of curiosity and conversation or a furious war against whichever side you think is evil.

For those more curious than martial, one useful path through this thicket is to look at areas where extremists and eccentrics from very different worlds are talking about the same subject. Such overlap is no guarantee of wisdom, but it's often a sign that there's something interesting going on.

Which brings me to the sex robots.

Well, actually, first it brings me to the case of Robin Hanson, a George Mason economist, libertarian and noted brilliant weirdo. Commenting on the recent terrorist violence in Toronto, in which a self-identified "incel" — that is, involuntary celibate — man sought retribution against women and society for denying him the fornication he felt that he deserved, Hanson offered this provocation: If we are concerned about the just distribution of property and money, why do we assume that the desire for some sort of sexual redistribution is inherently ridiculous?

After all, he wrote, "one might plausibly argue that those with much less access to sex suffer to a similar degree as those with low income, and might similarly hope to gain from organizing around this identity, to lobby for redistribution along this axis and to at least implicitly threaten violence if their demands are not met."

This argument was not well received by people closer to the mainstream than Professor Hanson, to put it mildly. A representative response from Slate's Jordan Weissmann, "Is Robin Hanson the Creepiest Economist in America?", cited the post along with some previous creepy forays to dismiss Hanson as a misogynist weirdo not that far removed from the franker misogyny of toxic online males.

But Hanson's post made me immediately think of a recent essay in The London Review of Books by Amia Srinivasan, "Does Anyone Have the Right To Sex?" Srinivasan, an Oxford philosophy professor, covered similar ground (starting with an earlier "incel" killer) but expanded the argument well beyond the realm of male chauvinists to consider groups with whom The London Review's left-leaning and feminist readers would have more natural sympathy — the overweight and disabled, minority groups treated as unattractive by the majority, trans women unable to find partners and other victims, in her narrative, of a society that still makes us prisoners of patriarchal and also racist-sexist-homophobic rules of sexual desire.

Srinivasan ultimately answered her title question in the negative: "There is no entitlement to sex, and everyone is entitled to want what they want." But her negative answer was a qualified one. While "no one has a right to be desired," at the same time "who is desired and who isn't is a political question," which left-wing and feminist politics might help society answer differently someday. This wouldn't instantiate a formal right to sex, exactly, but if the new order worked as its revolutionary architects intended, sex would be more justly distributed than it is today.

A number of the critics I saw engaging with Srinivasan's essay tended to respond the way a normal center-left writer like Weissmann engaged with Hanson's thought experiment — by commenting on its weirdness or ideological extremity rather than engaging fully with its substance. But to me, reading Hanson and Srinivasan together offers a good case study in how intellectual eccentrics — like socialists and populists in politics — can surface issues and problems that lurk beneath the surface of more mainstream debates.

By this I mean that as offensive or utopian the redistribution of sex might sound, the idea is entirely responsive to the logic of late-modern sexual life, and its pursuit would be entirely characteristic of a recurring pattern in liberal societies.

First, because like other forms of neoliberal deregulation the sexual revolution created new winners and losers, new hierarchies to replace the old ones, privileging the beautiful and rich and socially adept in new ways and relegating others to new forms of loneliness and frustration.

Second, because in this new landscape, and amid other economic and technological transformations, the sexes seem to be struggling generally to relate to one another, with social and political chasms opening between them and not only marriage and family but also sexual activity itself in recent decline.

Third, because the culture's dominant message about sex is still essentially Hefnerian, despite certain revisions attempted by feminists since the heyday of the Playboy philosophy — a message that frequency and variety in sexual experience is as close to a summum bonum as the human condition has to offer, that the greatest possible diversity in sexual desires and tastes and identities should be not only accepted but cultivated, and that virginity and celibacy are at best strange and at worst pitiable states. And this master narrative, inevitably, makes both the new inequalities and the decline of actual relationships that much more difficult to bear …

… which in turn encourages people, as ever under modernity, to place their hope for escape from the costs of one revolution in a further one yet to come, be it political, social or technological, which will supply if not the promised utopia at least some form of redress for the many people that progress has obviously left behind.

There is an alternative, conservative response, of course — namely, that our widespread isolation and unhappiness and sterility might be dealt with by reviving or adapting older ideas about the virtues of monogamy and chastity and permanence and the special respect owed to the celibate.

But this is not the natural response for a society like ours. Instead we tend to look for fixes that seem to build on previous revolutions, rather than reverse them.

In the case of sexual liberation and its discontents, that's unlikely to mean the kind of thoroughgoingly utopian reimagining of sexual desire that writers like Srinivasan think we should aspire toward, or anything quite so formal as the pro-redistribution political lobby of Hanson's thought experiment.

But I expect the logic of commerce and technology will be consciously harnessed, as already in pornography, to address the unhappiness of incels, be they angry and dangerous or simply depressed and despairing. The left's increasing zeal to transform prostitution into legalized and regulated "sex work" will have this end implicitly in mind, the libertarian (and general male) fascination with virtual-reality porn and sex robots will increase as those technologies improve — and at a certain point, without anyone formally debating the idea of a right to sex, right-thinking people will simply come to agree that some such right exists, and that it makes sense to look to some combination of changed laws, new technologies and evolved mores to fulfill it.

Whether sex workers and sex robots can actually deliver real fulfillment is another matter. But that they will eventually be asked to do it, in service to a redistributive goal that for now still seems creepy or misogynist or radical, feels pretty much inevitable.

ROSS DOUTHAT is an Op-Ed columnist for The New York Times.

The Boundary Between Abuse and B.D.S.M.

BY VALERIYA SAFRONOVA AND KATIE VAN SYCKLE | MAY 23, 2018

Politicians accused of abusing their sexual partners have put the community's practices in the news.

"YOU WANT TO MAKE SURE that you narrate what is going to be happening," a blond woman in a skintight nurse's costume said. She had just demonstrated how to safely, and consensually, stick a willing partner with hypodermic needles.

The subject of her class was "medical play" and the crowd was standing-room-only. The event was hosted by the Eulenspiegel Society in Manhattan, which describes itself as the "oldest and largest B.D.S.M. support and education group" in the country.

The "nurse," Margot, was not acting as a health care professional, though she did offer hygiene tips. She was there, with her role-play partner for the evening, June, to model best practices. (Many of those interviewed for this piece, including Margot and June, did not want to use their full or legal names for fear of stigma.)

"You create a container for the things that are your worst fears, your darkest fantasies, and you create very strong boundaries around that," Margot said. "Respecting those boundaries is the most important thing."

Those who practice bondage, dominance, sadism and masochism (B.D.S.M.) have rules for protecting boundaries, safety and consent. But the line between B.D.S.M. and abuse has been in the news after two politicians were accused of abusing their sexual partners.

In a report released in April, a woman accused Gov. Eric Greitens of Missouri of taping her hands to exercise equipment, hitting and shoving her, and touching her without her agreement. The woman also said she thought he had taken a photograph of her without her consent; charges brought on that account were withdrawn last week.

"This was a great victory and a long time coming. I've said from the beginning that I am innocent," Mr. Greitens tweeted. (The charges only addressed invasion of privacy.)

In May, four women told The New Yorker that Eric T. Schneiderman, then the New York attorney general, had assaulted them. Mr. Schneiderman defended himself by claiming he was participating in role play. He also said he wanted to "strongly contest" the claims, but that they would "effectively prevent me from leading the office's work at this critical time." He resigned hours after the investigation was published.

These situations bear little resemblance to consensual B.D.S.M. encounters, practitioners say. "There's no demarcation in these abuse situations," said Clarisse Thorn, author of "The S&M Feminist." Of the reported incidents between Mr. Schneiderman and the four women, she said, "What these women are reporting is, 'He would hit me without warning and he would keep going until he wanted to stop.' "

"There is a difference between abuse and B.D.S.M.," said Gigi, a spokesperson for the The Eulenspiegel Society. "That difference is consent."

WHAT IS 'SAFE, SANE AND CONSENSUAL'?

B.D.S.M. practitioners use the catchphrase "safe, sane and consensual" to summarize best practices for sexual encounters that mix with violence. Extensive conversations, negotiated checklists and safe words are tools for navigating consent.

Setting time constraints is also important, Ms. Thorn said, because most B.D.S.M. enthusiasts are not constantly "on." She provided an example of how time limits can be established: "We're going to do a scene right now," she said, referring to an episode of role play. "We'll demarcate that with one person wearing a collar and calling the other person 'sir,' and we'll do it this evening and when it's done, it's done."

The key, said Mollena Williams, a self-described submissive and author of "Playing Well With Others," is to "make a list of things that you absolutely need to have in order to feel safe, in order to feel heard, and then make a list of things that would be great if they happened."

'IT'S ALMOST LIKE A CHOOSE-YOUR-OWN-ADVENTURE.'

Lola Jean, a sex educator and mental health professional, said it is important to tailor each experience to individual preferences and not assume that there is any one-size-fits-all approach to B.D.S.M. "It's almost like a choose-your-own-adventure," she said.

Participants have to know — and be able to describe and set — their own limits. "I can take a lot of punching and kicking, but for whatever reason, if you slap my face, I go emotionally to pieces," said a longtime B.D.S.M. practitioner who goes by the name Ninja Juicer.

"It used to be you had a mentor," said Cassandra Moon, a Brooklynite who has long identified as a dominant woman. "Someone you go and hang out with and they would play with their partners and you would watch them do so."

Now, someone interested in B.D.S.M. might also go to a "munch," a plainclothes gathering where people with different sexual interests meet and mingle. Dungeons provide another space for people to interact and explore their desires. Those spaces have rules and safety monitors, often dressed in bright orange vests, who are on alert for the use of safe words.

"Within the scene, the person receiving always has an out, a safe word," Ms. Moon said. "If a safe word is used, then you stop everything immediately."

'YOU DO NOT BRING A MYSTERY IN.'

Safe words don't work for everyone. Other practices include making checklists in advance and nonverbal gestures, such as a pinch of the knee. Some checklists "have 1 to 5 scales for how into something you are," Ms. Thorn said. "If your partner is a 5 on being tied up and a 0 on face slapping, you can engage in B.D.S.M. while knowing very granular information about their boundaries."

Some B.D.S.M. practitioners criticize the use of contracts or apps that codify an agreement. Preferences change, they say, and no one should feel locked into agreements when their boundaries may change over time.

"You shouldn't bring in something that someone hasn't discussed with you," Ms. Moon said. "That's so important in this thing. You do not bring a mystery in."

"I went on a date with a vanilla guy, somebody who wasn't involved in the community, and in the middle of the scene he started choking me," a B.D.S.M. practitioner who goes by Salty Goodness said. "Luckily I felt safe enough and in a position to just be like, 'Whoa dude, note that we did not talk about that. That's not okay.'"

Members of the B.D.S.M. community also warn against partaking in violent sexual activity while drinking alcohol or taking drugs. "If you happen to have two vodka Martinis and you're about to suspend someone, you can cause serious damage," said a former professional dominatrix, who identified herself as Ms. Smiles. "Same thing if you're using a whip and your eye-hand coordination is being thrown off because you're under the influence."

'WE JUST REALLY LIKE TO BE ADVENTUROUS WITH OUR SEXUALITY.'

Legally, though, people can't consent to just anything.

"There's an important body of law that declares it illegal to consent to certain types of physical harm, whether it's sexual or not," said Wendy Murphy, a professor of sexual violence law at New England School of Law. "You can't consent to torture. You cannot consent to serious bodily injury."

Practically, this means that strangulation, cutting or burning a partner could be prosecuted by law enforcement as assault and battery or aggravated assault — even if the victim consented.

"People who are not interested in kinky sex find it hard to understand, but some of us are just wired to really enjoy extreme sensations, whether it's emotional or physical or mental challenge," said Susan Wright, the founder of the National Coalition for Sexual Freedom, an advocacy organization.

June, the woman leading the demonstration at The Eulenspiegel Society's class, said she enjoyed being poked with needles. "I have an elation, it is an endorphin rush that makes me proud of my body and what it can handle," she said.

"To understand you have a kink, you're already ahead of people," said Ms. Jean, the sex educator. "To act on it and explore it, that's the most noble thing. There's no confidence like knowing yourself."

VALERIYA SAFRONOVA is a reporter for the Style section. She is based in New York.

The Digital Sex Lives
of Young Gay Teenagers

OPINION | BY JACK TURBAN | JUNE 13, 2018

LAST SUMMER IN WISCONSIN, a mother came home to find her 15-year-old son running up the stairs from their basement. He yelled that a man had broken into the house and raped him. A police officer apprehended Eugene Gross, who was 51 years old and H.I.V. positive, in a nearby backyard.

Authorities later learned that the teenager had met Mr. Gross on the gay hookup app Grindr and that they had met for sex before. Last month, Mr. Gross was sentenced to 15 years. The victim's father broke down in court, saying, "The man sitting here, he destroyed my life, my kid's life, my family life."

It's common for gay, bisexual or questioning minors to go online to meet other gay people. It's normal for these kids to want to explore intimacy. But most online social networks for gay men are geared toward adults and focused on sex. They have failed to protect minors, who simply have to subtract a few years from their birth date to create a profile.

Data from the Centers for Disease Control and Prevention and a new study in The Journal of Adolescent Health together suggest that roughly one in four gay and bisexual boys aged 14 to 17 in the United States are on gay hookup apps designed for adults (Grindr, Scruff, Jack'd, Adam4Adam). Sixty-nine percent of them have had sex with someone they met through these apps. Only 25 percent use condoms consistently.

Gay kids, especially closeted ones, don't necessarily have the opportunities for intimacy that straight kids do: classroom Valentines and first prom dates. So they go online. Though they may be looking for friends or boyfriends, they mostly find sex.

On Grindr, it's common to receive unsolicited naked pictures. A minor can make a profile within minutes and instantly start chatting with adult men who live nearby.

Teenagers are still developing their abilities to delay gratification and control their impulses. With just 12 percent of millennials reporting that their sex education classes covered same-sex relationships, it's not surprising that many end up having unprotected sex.

Should apps like Grindr be held accountable when minors use them? Dr. Elizabeth Englander, a psychologist and expert on the digital lives of minors, thinks yes: "It's an ethical line and a no-brainer."

Grindr's terms of service state that users must be 18 or older, and the app requires everyone to enter a birth date to join. But it could certainly do more to try to verify ages. Some gambling sites, for instance, make users upload a credit card or ID to prove their age. But this brings up confidentiality risks for gay men who don't want to be outed.

Grindr could also use algorithms to detect conversations between minors and adults. This would require employees to manually verify which conversations were inappropriate, but given that Grindr's annual revenue may be as high as $77 million, the company could probably afford it.

When asked to comment, Grindr's chief technology officer and president, Scott Chen, said that Grindr is "in the process of testing further safeguards for our account creation procedures to help ensure authentic and proper account activity, including verification through social media platforms." He said the company takes the issue very seriously, is working on improving its screening tools and encourages users to continue reporting any "illegal or improper activity."

This is heartening, but it isn't enough. Age verification through social media is hardly foolproof, since minors can lie about their age on Facebook, too.

In 2015, a man who had been arrested for having sex with a 13-year-old boy sued Grindr, claiming that its weak enforcement of age restrictions was to blame for the sexual encounter. The lawsuit was dismissed because Grindr is protected by Section 230 of the Communications Decency Act, which means it isn't responsible for what users say on its app (including minors lying about their age).

And Grindr is hardly the only problem — there are many similar venues. When I searched online for "gay chat," as a lonely, closeted child might, the first hit was #1 Chat Avenue. Two minutes after I opened a gay chat room, a user wrote: "Any boys 13 or 14 with cameras? I'm 35." After some deep searching, I found that you can report activity like this to moderators, but they aren't always online. I reported it to the site's administrator via email, but I never heard back.

In the end, it is largely up to parents to protect their children. Unfortunately, this topic combines two of many parents' greatest fears: sex and technology.

Parents can block apps like Grindr. But kids almost always outsmart us, and it's probably better to educate them in addition to using parental controls.

Dr. Englander tells parents not to try to be experts on the technology. "Parents can instead be the experts on the importance of deeper in-person relationships," she says. Explain to children that while what they find online may be exciting or interesting, they never know who's on the other side.

Children need to hear that naked photos and videos are permanent (even when sent on Snapchat). They should know that sex between a minor and an adult is illegal. They need to be told that it's dangerous to meet up with a person from the internet and that if they do so, they need to tell their parents and meet the person in a public place. They need to know the risk of infections from unprotected sex.

Parents also need to stay calm, so that the kids feel comfortable coming back to them if they ever end up in a bad situation, like if a scary stranger won't stop messaging.

As a society, we have failed to create enough spaces for gay youth to thrive, pushing them online and underground. While we try to find ways to hold digital sites accountable, we need to talk to our kids about how to be safe online.

JACK TURBAN (@jack_turban) is a resident physician in psychiatry at Massachusetts General Hospital and McLean Hospital.

Glossary

asexual A sexual orientation defined by a lack of sexual feelings, desires or associations.

bisexual Sexually attracted to both men and women.

cisgender Relating to a person whose sense of identity and gender corresponds with the sex they were assigned at birth.

consent Explicit permission given by someone allowing something to happen.

feminism The advocacy of women's rights on the basis of political, social and economic equality to men.

gay A term that primarily refers to a person (especially a male) who expresses same-sex attraction.

gender dysphoria The condition of feeling one's gender identity as different than or opposite to one's biological sex.

gender identity A person's internal sense of their gender. For transgender people, this may not match the sex they were assigned at birth.

gender-nonconforming Relating to a person whose behavior, appearance or identity does not conform to social conventions relating to their gender.

heterosexual Sexually attracted to people of the opposite sex.

intersectionality A theory that argues that the overlap of social identities contributes to the specific type of oppression or discrimination experienced by an individual.

intersex A term used to define a person who is born with sexual or reproductive anatomy that doesn't fit into typical gender characteristics.

lesbian A term referring to a woman who experiences sexual, romantic or emotional attraction to other women.

marginalization The treatment of a person or group as insignificant or unimportant.

non-binary A category that refers to gender identities that are not exclusively masculine or feminine.

pansexual Not limited in sexual choice or attraction with regard to biological sex, gender or gender identity.

polyamorous A relationship status in which an individual loves or is engaged in sexual acts with multiple partners.

queer An umbrella term that encompasses sexual and gender minorities who are not heterosexual or cisgender.

transgender Relating to a person whose sense of gender identity does not correspond with the sex they were assigned at birth.

transvestite A person who derives pleasure from dressing in clothes associated with the opposite sex.

Media Literacy Terms

"Media literacy" refers to the ability to access, understand, critically assess and create media. The following terms are important components of media literacy, and they will help you critically engage with the articles in this title.

angle The aspect of a news story that a journalist focuses on and develops.

balance Principle of journalism that both perspectives of an argument should be presented in a fair way.

bias A disposition of prejudice in favor of a certain idea, person or perspective.

column A type of story that is a regular feature, often on a recurring topic, written by the same journalist, generally known as a columnist.

commentary A type of story that is an expression of opinion on recent events by a journalist generally known as a commentator.

credibility The quality of being trustworthy and believable, said of a journalistic source.

editorial Article of opinion or interpretation.

feature story Article designed to entertain as well as to inform.

human interest story A type of story that focuses on individuals and how events or issues affect their life, generally offering a sense of relatability to the reader.

impartiality Principle of journalism that a story should not reflect a journalist's bias and should contain balance.

intention The motive or reason behind something, such as the publication of a news story.

interview story A type of story in which the facts are gathered primarily by interviewing another person or persons.

motive The reason behind something, such as the publication of a news story or a source's perspective on an issue.

news story An article or style of expository writing that reports news, generally in a straightforward fashion and without editorial comment.

op-ed An opinion piece that reflects a prominent individual's opinion on a topic of interest.

paraphrase The summary of an individual's words, with attribution, rather than a direct quotation of their exact words.

plagiarism An attempt to pass another person's work as one's own without attribution.

quotation The use of an individual's exact words indicated by the use of quotation marks and proper attribution.

reliability The quality of being dependable and accurate, said of a journalistic source.

rhetorical device Technique in writing intending to persuade the reader or communicate a message from a certain perspective.

source The origin of the information reported in journalism.

style A distinctive use of language in writing or speech; also a news or publishing organization's rules for consistent use of language with regards to spelling, punctuation, typography and capitalization, usually regimented by a house style guide.

tone A manner of expression in writing or speech.

Media Literacy Questions

1. Identify the various sources cited in the article "Who Is a Feminist Now?" (on page 138). How does Marisa Meltzer attribute information to each of these sources in her article? How effective are her attributions in helping the reader identify her sources?

2. In "For Young Gays on the Streets, Survival Comes Before Pride; Few Beds for Growing Class of Homeless" (on page 23), Andrew Jacobs paraphrases information from David Antoine. What are the strengths of the use of a paraphrase as opposed to a direct quote? What are the weaknesses?

3. Compare the headlines of "After Sex Change, Teacher Is Barred From School" (on page 50) and "Watershed of Mourning at the Border of Gender" (on page 54). Which is a more compelling headline, and why? How could the less compelling headline be changed to better draw the reader's interest?

4. What type of story is "The Patriarchs Are Falling. The Patriarchy Is Stronger Than Ever." (on page 159)? Can you identify another article in this collection that is the same type of story?

5. Does Benedict Carey demonstrate the journalistic principle of balance in his article "Straight, Gay or Lying? Bisexuality Revisited" (on page 98)? If so, how did he do so? If not, what could Carey have included to make his article more balanced?

6. The article "The Redistribution of Sex" (on page 198) is an example of an op-ed. Identify how Ross Douthat's attitude and tone help convey his opinion on the topic.

7. Does "Solace and Fury as Schools React to Transgender Policy" (on page 68) use multiple sources? What are the strengths of using multiple sources in a journalistic piece? What are the weaknesses of relying heavily on only one or a few sources?

8. What is the intention of the article "If You're Asking, 'Am I Gay? Lesbian? Bi? Trans? Queer?' Here's a Start" (on page 111)? How effectively does it achieve its intended purpose?

9. Analyze the authors' reporting in "Morals: On the Third Sex" (on page 10) and "The Woman Homosexual: More Assertive, Less Willing to Hide" (on page 81). Do you think one journalist is more impartial in their reporting than the other? If so, why do you think so?

10. Identify each of the sources in "Generation LGBTQIA" (on page 103) as a primary source or a secondary source. Evaluate the reliability and credibility of each source. How does your evaluation of each source change your perspective on this article?

11. "Queer Love in Color" (on page 124) features several photographs. What do these photographs add to the article?

Citations

All citations in this list are formatted according to the Modern Language Association's (MLA) style guide.

BOOK CITATION

THE NEW YORK TIMES EDITORIAL STAFF. *Sex and Sexuality*. New York: New York Times Educational Publishing, 2019.

ONLINE ARTICLE CITATIONS

ARONOWITZ, NONA WILLIS. "The Feminist Pursuit of Good Sex." *The New York Times*, 16 Feb. 2018, https://www.nytimes.com/2018/02/16/opinion/sunday/feminist-pursuit-good-sex.html.

BARRON, JAMES. "Homosexuals See 2 Decades of Gains, but Fear Setbacks." *The New York Times*, 25 June 1989, www.nytimes.com/1989/06/25/nyregion/homosexuals-see-2-decades-of-gains-but-fear-setbacks.html.

BATURA, AMBER. "How Hugh Hefner Invented the Modern Man." *The New York Times*, 28 Sept. 2017, https://www.nytimes.com/2017/09/28/opinion/hugh-hefner-playboy.html.

BENNETT, JESSICA. "When a Feminist Pledges a Sorority." *The New York Times*, 9 Apr. 2016, https://www.nytimes.com/2016/04/10/fashion/sorority-ivy-league-feminists.html.

BILTON, NICK. "Tinder, the Fast-Growing Dating App, Taps an Age-Old Truth." *The New York Times*, 29 Oct. 2014, https://www.nytimes.com/2014/10/30/fashion/tinder-the-fast-growing-dating-app-taps-an-age-old-truth.html.

BLOOM, JULIE. "Sexuality and Other Female (Film) Troubles." *The New York Times*, 11 May 2012, https://www.nytimes.com/2012/05/13/movies/sexuality-and-other-female-film-troubles.html.

BOYLAN, JENNIFER FINNEY. "Why Scarlett Johansson Shouldn't Play a Trans Man." *The New York Times*, 6 July 2018, https://www.nytimes.com/2018/07/06/opinion/why-scarlett-johansson-shouldnt-play-a-trans-man.html.

BROWN, PATRICIA LEIGH. "A Quest for a Restroom That's Neither Men's Room Nor Women's Room." *The New York Times*, 4 Mar. 2005, https://www.nytimes.com/2005/03/04/us/a-quest-for-a-restroom-thats-neither-mens-room-nor-womens-room.html.

CAREY, BENEDICT. "Straight, Gay or Lying? Bisexuality Revisited." *The New York Times*, 5 July 2005, https://www.nytimes.com/2005/07/05/health/straight-gay-or-lying-bisexuality-revisited.html.

CRISPIN, JESSA. "What to Ask a Celebrity Instead of 'Are You a Feminist?'" *The New York Times*, 25 Feb. 2017, https://www.nytimes.com/2017/02/25/opinion/sunday/what-to-ask-a-celebrity-instead-of-are-you-a-feminist.html.

DOUTHAT, ROSS. "The Redistribution of Sex." *The New York Times*, 2 May 2018, https://www.nytimes.com/2018/05/02/opinion/incels-sex-robots-redistribution.html.

DUNLAP, DAVID W. "Gay Parents Ease Into Suburbia; For the First Generation, Car Pools and Soccer Games." *The New York Times*, 16 May 1996, www.nytimes.com/1996/05/16/garden/gay-parents-ease-into-suburbia-for-first-generation-car-pools-soccer-games.html.

EDDY, MELISSA, AND JESSICA BENNETT. "Germany Must Allow Third Gender Category, Court Rules." *The New York Times*, 8 Nov. 2017, https://www.nytimes.com/2017/11/08/world/europe/germany-third-gender-category-vanja.html.

FALUDI, SUSAN. "The Patriarchs Are Falling. The Patriarchy Is Stronger Than Ever." *The New York Times*, 28 Dec. 2017, https://www.nytimes.com/2017/12/28/opinion/sunday/patriarchy-feminism-metoo.html.

HARWOOD, JOHN. "A Sea Change in Less Than 50 Years as Gay Rights Gained Momentum." *The New York Times*, 26 Mar. 2013, www.nytimes.com/2013/03/26/us/in-less-than-50-years-a-sea-change-on-gay-rights.html.

HEALY, JACK, AND RICHARD PÉREZ-PEÑA. "Solace and Fury as Schools React to Transgender Policy." *The New York Times*, 13 May 2016, https://www.nytimes.com/2016/05/14/us/transgender-bathrooms.html.

JACOBS, ANDREW. "For Young Gays on the Streets, Survival Comes Before Pride; Few Beds for Growing Class of Homeless." *The New York Times*, 27 June 2004, www.nytimes.com/2004/06/27/nyregion/for-young-gays-streets-survival-comes-before-pride-few-beds-for-growing-class.html.

JORDAN, JAMAL. "Queer Love in Color." *The New York Times*, 21 June 2018, https://www.nytimes.com/2018/06/21/us/queer-love-in-color.html.

KLEMESRUD, JUDY. "The Lesbian Issue and Women's Lib." *The New York*

Times, 18 Dec. 1970, https://www.nytimes.com/1970/12/18/archives/the -lesbian-issue-and-womens-lib.html.

LIPTAK, ADAM. "Supreme Court Ruling Makes Same-Sex Marriage a Right Nationwide." *The New York Times*, 26 June 2015, https://www.nytimes .com/2015/06/27/us/supreme-court-same-sex-marriage.html.

LONDOÑO, ERNESTO. "Increasingly Visible, Transgender Americans Defy Stereotypes." *The New York Times*, 18 May 2015, https://www.nytimes .com/2015/05/18/opinion/increasingly-visible-transgender-americans -defy-stereotypes.html.

LOORY, STUART H. "Surgery to Change Gender." *The New York Times*, 27 Nov. 1966, https://timesmachine.nytimes.com/timesmachine/1966 /11/27/296412802.pdf.

MEDINA, JENNIFER. "California May Require Teaching of Gay History." *The New York Times*, 15 Apr. 2011, https://www.nytimes.com/2011/04/16/us /16schools.html.

MELTZER, MARISA. "Who Is a Feminist Now?" *The New York Times*, 21 May 2014, https://www.nytimes.com/2014/05/22/fashion/who-is-a-feminist-now.html.

NAGOURNEY, ADAM. "Political Shifts on Gay Rights Lag Behind Culture." *The New York Times*, 27 June 2009, www.nytimes.com/2009/06/28/us /28stonewall.html.

NEMY, ENID. "Group Sex: Is It 'Life Art' or a Sign That Something Is Wrong?" *The New York Times*, 10 May 1971, https://www.nytimes.com/1971/05/10 /archives/group-sex-is-it-life-art-or-a-sign-that-something-is-wrong.html.

NEMY, ENID. "The Woman Homosexual: More Assertive, Less Willing to Hide." *The New York Times*, 17 Nov. 1969, https://timesmachine.nytimes .com/timesmachine/1969/11/17/89384506.html.

THE NEW YORK TIMES. " 'Deviates' and 'Inverts.' " *The New York Times*, 11 Apr. 2009, www.nytimes.com/2009/04/12/weekinreview/12liptakbox.html.

THE NEW YORK TIMES. "Transsexual Tries to Build a New Life." *The New York Times*, 20 Nov. 1972, https://timesmachine.nytimes.com/timesmachine /1972/11/20/90730876.pdf.

NIEVES, EVELYN. "After Sex Change, Teacher Is Barred From School." *The New York Times*, 27 Sept. 1999, https://www.nytimes.com/1999/09/27/us /after-sex-change-teacher-is-barred-from-school.html.

NORTH, ANNA. "Should 'Slut' Be Retired?" *The New York Times*, 3 Feb. 2015, https://op-talk.blogs.nytimes.com/2015/02/03/should-slut-be-retired.

ORENSTEIN, PEGGY. "What Makes a Woman a Woman?" *The New York Times*,

11 Sept. 2009, https://www.nytimes.com/2009/09/13/magazine
/13FOB-WWLN-t.html.

PHILIPPS, DAVE. "Ban Was Lifted, but Transgender Recruits Still Can't Join
Up." *The New York Times*, 5 July 2018, https://www.nytimes.com/2018
/07/05/us/military-transgender-recruits.html.

PORIZKOVA, PAULINA. "America Made Me a Feminist." *The New York Times*,
10 June 2017, https://www.nytimes.com/2017/06/10/opinion/sunday
/paulina-porizkova-america-feminist.html.

SAFRONOVA, VALERIYA, AND KATIE VAN SYCKLE. "The Boundary Between Abuse
and B.D.S.M." *The New York Times*, 23 May 2018, https://www.nytimes
.com/2018/05/23/style/bdsm-kink-consent.html.

SALAM, MAYA. "If You're Asking, 'Am I Gay? Lesbian? Bi? Trans? Queer?'
Here's a Start." *The New York Times*, 17 May 2017, https://www.nytimes
.com/2017/05/17/smarter-living/gay-lesbian-bisexual-transgender.html.

SCHULMAN, MICHAEL. "Generation LGBTQIA." *The New York Times*, 9 Jan. 2013,
https://www.nytimes.com/2013/01/10/fashion/generation-lgbtqia.html.

SCHUMACH, MURRAY. "Morals: On the Third Sex." *The New York Times*,
7 May 1967, https://timesmachine.nytimes.com/timesmachine/1967
/05/07/83597083.pdf.

SIEGAL, NINA. "Watershed of Mourning at the Border of Gender." *The New
York Times*, 24 July 2000, https://www.nytimes.com/2000/07/24/nyregion
/watershed-of-mourning-at-the-border-of-gender.html.

STEINEM, GLORIA. "March 22, 1998: Why Feminists Support Clinton." *The New
York Times*, 25 Sept. 2010, https://www.nytimes.com/2010/09/26/opinion
/eq-steinem.html.

TURBAN, JACK. "The Digital Sex Lives of Young Gay Teenagers." *The New York
Times*, 13 June 2018, https://www.nytimes.com/2018/06/13/opinion
/grindr-gay-teenagers-sex-apps.html.

WILGOREN, JODI. "Suit Over Estate Claims a Widow Is Not a Woman." *The New
York Times*, 13 Jan. 2002, https://www.nytimes.com/2002/01/13/us
/suit-over-estate-claims-a-widow-is-not-a-woman.html.

WORTHAM, JENNA. "When Everyone Can Be 'Queer,' Is Anyone?" *The New
York Times*, 12 July 2016, https://www.nytimes.com/2016/07/17/magazine
/when-everyone-can-be-queer-is-anyone.html.

Index

Rustin, Bayard, 32

S

same-sex marriage, 7, 14, 27, 30, 36, 37, 38–43
Sandberg, Sheryl, 139, 195
Santana, Harmony, 64, 66–67
Saunders, Dave, 29
Scalia, Antonin, 39, 40, 41, 43
Scherker, Michael, 19
Schwarzenegger, Arnold, 32, 62
Second Wave feminist movement, 131, 194–197
Seidman, Rachel F., 142
Sell, Randall, 99
Semenya, Caster, 135, 137
Siciliano, Carl, 24
Silverman, Michael, 71
Singer, Laura, 166
Socarides, Charles W., 84, 87, 88
Socarides, Richard, 31
sodomy laws, 7, 11, 20, 21
sororities, and feminism, 143–152
Sparta, 73, 74
Stack, Melissa, 138
Stacy, Nancy, 70
St. Laurent, Octavia, 56
Stoddard, Thomas B., 20
Stonewall Inn, raid on, 10, 13, 16, 18–19, 20, 22, 28, 33, 34, 65

Street Transvestite Action Revolutionaries, 65
Stryker, Susan, 64
Student Homophile League, 82, 88–89
suicide, 24, 32, 48, 53, 88, 115
Sullivan, Lou, 66
surgery to change gender, 8, 44–47, 48, 49, 50–53, 54, 57, 61, 65, 66, 108
Symonds, Carolyn, 165

T

Tambor, Jeffrey, 79
Tanenbaum, Leora, 183, 184, 186, 187, 188
Tanis, Farah, 186, 187
Tedesco, Jeremy, 70
Thomas More Center for Law and Justice, 58
Thorn, Clarisse, 203, 204
Tinder, 178–182
Transcending Gender, 66
transgender Americans, increased visibility of, 64–67
Transgender Law Center, 62
Trans Lifeline, 115
"Transvestia," 65
Trevor Project, 115
Trump, Donald/Trump administration, 72, 74, 75, 76, 155, 159, 160, 163
TSQ: Transgender Studies

Quarterly, 64
Turk, Diana, 149

U

United States v. Windsor, 40

V

violence/assaults, 8, 9, 13, 17, 23, 24, 44, 54–56, 60, 61, 62, 114, 145, 148, 151, 163, 187, 197, 198, 199, 203, 205
Vitale, Jeffrey J., 92

W

Warfield, David, 50–53
Washington, Eric, 18
Weiner, Jennifer, 138
Weinstein, Harvey, 9, 159, 160
Wexler, Tanya, 174–177
White, Edward, 58
Wilchins, Riki, 61
Wilson, Jamia A., 184, 185, 186–187, 188
Windmeyer, Shane, 104
Woodley, Shailene, 138, 139, 140, 142
World Professional Association for Transgender Health, 115
Wright, Io Tillett, 111, 112, 113, 114, 115–116

Z

Zeisler, Andi, 139, 140

This book is current up until the time of printing. For the most up-to-date reporting, visit www.nytimes.com.